DIVORCE TO
DISCOVERY

JILL WILSON

BEAR PRESS

ISBN: 978-1-999-884246
A CIP record for this book is available
from the British Library

For Bear Press
Editors: Donna Rawlings
Bridget Scrannage
Sarah Fish
Art Director: Sarah Joy
Cover Illustration: Ian Scrannage

Technical information about this book
is available at www.bearpress.uk/isbn

Set in 11/15pt PT Serif

1v05

For my dear sister
Jackie,
thank you for your
inspiration and guidance.

Foreword

by Fern Britton

Jill has written a truly inspirational book. When I first met her, she was a woman coming out of a long marriage with no idea of what the future held for her. In a moment's madness she put herself forward for a challenge, one of three that we at *This Morning* had decided on for women who needed to shake themselves. Find themselves. Something to jolt them out of their lives. To get them going again. To give them a fresh perspective.

One challenge was to run the London Marathon; one to swim the Channel; and the third was a cycle ride through Rajasthan, India. 400km in baking heat and high humidity with little sanitation, wild goats and mad dogs.

We selected Jill for that one!

Some of it was very luxurious – first class plane seats and cars – but otherwise this was the chance to see India in all its raw and earthy vitality – such a wonderful country and one that I fell in love with – the colours, the spirit of its people and the food.

Unfortunately Jill didn't like Indian food – challenge number one!

This is the story of her resilience and her determination to get the best out of her life – I hope you enjoy it.

Contents

PART THREE – AFTER INDIA

Introduction

"I want to know what it's like not to be married." These words from my husband ended my marriage of thirty-six years and started me on a long road to self-discovery which led me from devastation to happiness.

Just like that, my husband, in whose footsteps I'd trodden faithfully for those thirty-six years, had gone. He'd decided that he wanted a divorce. I'd always followed his direction and ideas, the faithful wife who worked so hard behind the scenes: in his shadow, always in his shadow. *What on earth was I going to do?*

Once I began to emerge from the emotional abyss of divorce, my attitude changed and I started to see my life in a different light. Instead of feeling like a victim, I saw myself as an active participant in our marriage and its undoing. I took responsibility for what had happened to me during that time. I learnt that I'm incredibly strong and independent. The illusion that I was incapable of taking care of myself was just that, an illusion. To understand why, I've had to dig deep into my past.

Sometimes very painful, sometimes with its funny side, this is my story of what I did and how I now cast my own shadow. That's something of which I'm very proud. It always reminds me that the struggle to find myself was so worthwhile and uplifting in the end. I feel a bit like a butterfly that has emerged from its chrysalis into the sunshine. I've written this story from my heart but aimed to remain objective. Although I was bitter when I started writing, I've tried hard to avoid being acrimonious, and hope I've achieved that.

I'm starting my story at a point in my life that's had a tremendous impact on me and is fundamental in showing how I took charge of myself. I was chosen as one of ten women to undertake 'The Challenge of Your Life' with ITV's

This Morning programme. Four of us would run the London Marathon, four would swim the English Channel, and two would cycle across Northern India with Fern Britton, one of the programme's presenters. After only three months of preparation the time had come to face my challenge – I was about to cycle from Fatehpur Sikri to Jaipur – approximately 420km.

A butterfly on a bicycle – oh, what a thought!

PART ONE

INDIA

Chapter 1 – The point of no return
Friday, 17 November 2006

Looking back, I don't recall a moment in my life where time totally stood still, but it was happening to me now. Blind panic froze me to the spot. It wasn't a particularly convenient spot to be frozen to, as it was right at the top of a set of steps leading out of an aircraft, and I was supposed to be walking down them. My brain was in turmoil, questioning why I was there. It wouldn't allow my feet to move. I kept telling myself to get a grip. I understood why I was there and what I'd achieved to get me to this point. It was far too late to turn back but I was feeling close to losing it completely. The point of no return had arrived.

This feeling started as I was preparing to leave the plane and step into the light. The heat was oppressive. There were alien smells and the noises were all so different. Standing there with tears stinging my eyes, I knew that if I started to cry I might not be able to stop. *What was I doing?* I just wanted to get back on the plane and go home. Only I didn't have a home to go to as I was currently living with my brother and his wife, and, after all, it was down to me that I was here in the first place.

In the past, it had never been me who'd decided what I was going to do; I'd always followed my husband's wishes and wants. Now that he was gone and the decisions were solely mine, I was petrified. However, this time, something told me I'd be able to accomplish this challenge. Where did this newfound strength and determination come from? Wherever that was, it still didn't stop me feeling very frightened. I wished it were possible to go and buy the few pounds of backbone that I now needed so much. Unfortunately, these things can't be bought; they come from within.

So, why was I in a blind panic? What had possessed me to

become part of a cycle ride across a large swathe of India? I was a middle-aged woman who'd spent most of her life in a long marriage. The mother of two grown-up, married daughters, and a grandmother. A well-organised and controlled woman, who was now looking at India from the top of those aircraft steps. Whatever I'd done to be there was in the past and I had no alternative but to get on with it, although my legs were telling me something different.

What have I done? I was in a strange land. I felt vulnerable and frightened – certainly not in control. I was completely out of my comfort zone, paralysed and unable to move. I'd always needed the carefully structured scaffolding that was around me – my family, my security and support. If that support wasn't there, how would I survive? Sheer terror was setting in.

***

Two days previously I'd been lying in my warm bed in England in the early hours of the morning listening to the rain drumming against the window. Everything was ready after endless packing. The day I'd imagined for the last three months had finally dawned. Suddenly, I started to worry about the enormity of what I'd taken on. I felt so nervous. I'd been brave and unfaltering up until that point. Was I just out to prove something to myself and other people? Lying in the darkness, hearing the rain, I thought about how things would be for the next eleven days. Uncomfortable beds, different food, hot weather and the dangers of monkeys with rabies. There would also be my biggest fear – snakes and spiders. I value my comfort so highly. *What was I doing?* What about not being able to put on my make-up every day, having a film crew following us, and, worst of all, *This Morning* viewers seeing me as I really was.

I had drifted off to sleep for a few hours and awoke again around 7.00am. A driver was due to pick me up at 3.30pm. He arrived an hour early, so after giving him a mug of tea and a bun, he said he'd get his head down in the car for a while as he'd had an early start that day. This gave me time to finish my late lunch and collect my thoughts. Then my holdall was loaded and I said a tearful goodbye to my family.

Was I really going through with this? I'd spent my whole life saying yes, I can do anything, but when it came to the crunch I always backed out, fearing I'd fail and make a fool of myself, or maybe I didn't have enough self-confidence to carry out the task. Had I thought that maybe I'd do the training and everything else involved, but then back out of doing the actual event at the last minute, as I usually did? There was something different this time. I knew I'd succeed. *Where did that come from?* Some place buried within me. Yet another veneer peeled back to find new strength and determination.

My chauffeur drove me to Heathrow Airport and wished me well. I pushed my trolley laden with luggage into the terminal. Susie, my cycling partner for this adventure, was already there and we met a few of the other ladies taking part in the Women for Women ride, one of whom was my training buddy from the Isle of Man. Women for Women and 'The Challenge of Your Life' cycle ride across India were being run on a combined basis. We met the film crew who would be travelling with us across Rajasthan, plus of course Fern Britton and Julie Dawn Cole, my mentor and fitness trainer. There was also a small team of people from *This Morning. Was I really going to India?* I kept pinching myself. The closer I got to that moment of getting on the aircraft and taking off, the more my stomach fluttered.

We were upgraded to first class. That meant we checked in very quickly. I felt like a film star. The first-class lounge resembled a five-star hotel. Adjusting my posture and tucking in my tummy, I attempted to glide in. This proved difficult, armed as I was with my saddle, helmet, and backpack, which we were allowed to include as hand luggage. The thought of losing that saddle after training on it for so long didn't bear thinking about.

There was champagne, caviar, cocktails, and an amazing selection of canapés. On several delicatessen counters, a shining array of foods was beautifully decorated. Each morsel beckoned me to sample it. I wondered whether my film-star image would be shattered if I sneaked some of this luxurious feast into my bum-bag in case hunger struck halfway across India.

In one corner was a massage suite, equipped with a few private rooms for full body massage and an open area at the front with several reclining leather chairs for masseurs to work on neck, shoulders, feet, and hands. I had my feet placed in a bowl of scented water. Next, soft clay was rubbed into them, then they were rinsed and patted dry with one of those very soft towels, finishing with a fragrant oil massage. I could get used to this.

At around 8.00pm, we were escorted to departures, then on to the plane. Individual cubicles, beds, duvets, champagne flowing, linen table cloths and napkins. We were given sleep suits and socks. Blimey, is this how the other half live?

Dinner consisted of chicken with an onion and sage herb crust, roast potatoes, carrots, broccoli, and traditional gravy, all served on bone china. I was being spoiled. I then began to wonder why. *Was this challenge going to be that awful?* I watched a film, settled down, and had a restless night's sleep. I awoke with a very dry mouth but recovered after a breakfast of fresh orange juice, cereal, fruit, croissant, and jam. I washed and changed, and then had a cup of tea as I looked out through the cabin portholes. The sun was so bright. The safety belt sign came on as we were about to land at Indira Gandhi International Airport in New Delhi. I adjusted my watch to local time: 4.45am became 10.15am. Well, here we go. I took a deep breath and headed for the door. That's when it really hit me.

Chapter 2 – So it begins

Those few seconds at the top of the aircraft step seemed like hours, but eventually passed. Time started to tick again. I pulled myself together and somehow descended from the aircraft. I had really started now and time for panic was over. I had to concentrate on what was happening and nothing else. Whatever was going on in my life before and however awful I'd felt, this was a new chapter beginning. It was exciting. We collected our luggage, re-grouped with the other women we were cycling with, and were then sectioned off into groups. Each group was named after an Indian god or goddess. Ours was the yellow group 'Ganesha', named after the Hindu god of new beginnings and remover of obstacles. We were herded on to a coach.

That journey will stick in my mind forever. We travelled from New Delhi to Agra, which should have taken five hours. In the end it took over six. The road surface was cracked and potholed. Carts filled with mountains of goods pulled by camels blocked the traffic. The camels glided along with an air of disdain, oblivious of the disruption they were causing. The sun was hot, and the dust was suffocating. This was apparently a major road! That didn't bode well for the minor roads and tracks we would be cycling along. My bike wouldn't need a saddle – a double cushion and back rest would be more in keeping. The driver of our coach was an absolute maniac. I remember thinking it was a wonder we weren't involved in an accident.

The noise around us was incredible. Radios and loudspeakers blared out in the most unlikely places. There was a baffling mixture of smells from richly pungent to delicately subtle. There were many beggars, some so physically handicapped they were distressing to look at. People used the streets like public conveniences, without any reservations about privacy. I was amazed by it all. It was too much to take in. One man was riding a bicycle with two goats on the back and yet another had his bike precariously piled at least four feet high with cages of squawking chickens. There were roadside vendors with huge vats of steaming food; taxis, cars, and buses full to bursting. It seemed as if they were all competing to get the highest number of people into a four-wheeled vehicle. The aroma of roasted peanuts, curry, and rubbish intermingled. Duelling motorists beeped their horns at each other continuously. It went from the extremes of cows walking in the road, to awe-inspiring palaces and forts. One minute smartly dressed people and the next, beggars with no legs, all shrouded in a low-hung mist caused by pollution. It was mind blowing. I wish there had been a pause button – in that way I could have moved it on slowly, so as not to miss a single sight.

After three hours of bumping around in the old worn-out coach with a driver who I was convinced had grown 'devil horns' during the journey, we stopped at a beautiful hotel for lunch. Where did this serene haven come from in the midst of this disorganised hubbub? On entering the grounds, we were sprinkled with the most amazing scented flower petals. The proprietors had provided a troupe of Indian dancers for entertainment. I vividly remember the meal. It was a curry buffet, the first of many, eaten in picturesque and peaceful grounds.

After eventually arriving in Agra, we pulled into the hotel which we would be staying in for two nights. We alighted from the coach and each of us was presented with a garland of sweet smelling jasmine. Another curry buffet in the evening, then a quick briefing of the following day's arrangements and off to bed.

Early the next morning, after a quick shower, we had a rather odd breakfast consisting of cold porridge, no sugar, a piece of rather peculiar bread, jam, and a cup of tea with hot milk. The milk was decidedly off. Then back to the boneshaker of a coach we'd been on the previous day. Thankfully we had a day to relax before our bike ride began, and we were off for some sight-seeing. Luckily we had a different driver who was slightly less homicidal. Our destination was the Taj Mahal, but the coach didn't take us all the way. Once we were close, we were transferred to what I can only describe as small milk floats called 'Tuk-Tuks' – three-wheeled scooters with passenger seating on the back. These ferried us to the door.

Hundreds of tourists flocked towards the entrance. There was an inevitable throng of beggars – children crying with outstretched hands and pleading eyes asking for money. Some were fake and well rehearsed; others seemed sadly real and my heart went out to them.

That first sight of the Taj Mahal filled me with one all-prevailing emotion, sadness, not for its history, but for me. The iconic picture of Diana, Princess of Wales, on the bench in front of this truly magnificent edifice came flooding into my mind. She looked sad, and now I think I can understand why. Not because she was by herself, more for what this monument symbolised: the expression of the total and undeniable love of a man for a woman. *Why hadn't I been able to inspire that kind of love?*

This beautiful building rising in its virginal whiteness from the baseness of everyday life inspires reflection. Every person entering the inner sanctum of the Taj Mahal was made to remove their shoes and given a pair of socks to wear so as not to sully the floor. This building had taken twenty-two years to construct as a symbolic declaration of devotion from one man to his bride. *Where was my Taj Mahal? Where were the declarations of love that I had craved for so long?* My tears flowed for a while.

We boarded our coach, then back to the hotel for lunch – more curry.

Some of the afternoon was spent getting 'fitted' to our new bikes. I decided I'd call my bike 'Soli' after my faithful machine at home. There would still, of course, be a very important part of 'Soli' on my new bike: his saddle. Thank heavens. Next was another visit, this time to the Pink Fort in Agra, finishing with a trip to the markets for a spot of shopping, then back to the hotel for dinner. Yes, it was curry.

That evening we had another briefing to cover the first day of our ride. I was scared. I'm not sure that another curry was the best dish to be having whilst feeling that way.

The team of bicycle mechanics travelling with us were to take our bikes to the start line in the village of Khanuan in the early hours of the morning.

The next day we transferred by coach from Agra to Fatehpur Sikri "City of Victory", which apparently had been the capital of the Mughal Empire. We had an all-too-brief forty-five minutes to walk around this historic city, and then boarded coaches to Khanuan for the start of our five-day cycle. Before embarking on our ride, a holy man conducted a Puja ceremony, asking the god Ganesha to bless our journey through the Rajasthan countryside. God of new beginnings – the opening of doors to a new life. Very appropriate for me I thought. The *sadhu* marked my forehead with a red symbol as a sign that I'd been blessed. This ceremony made me feel so emotional. I was again shedding more tears. So many thoughts and feelings – lonely, vulnerable, and very scared. The list was endless. *Could I do this?*

Chapter 3 – Day One: On the bike

Fatehpur Sikri to Campsite Bhusawar
Sunday, 19 November 2006

The first day's ride was on pothole-strewn secondary roads through endless tiny villages, sometimes passing the occasional temple. Our target was seventy-three kilometres to reach our overnight camp near the village of Bhusawar.

I had carried yellow ribbon from home for luck and I carefully attached it to my bike before we set out. How else could I recognise Soli? The ninety bikes were all new, the same colour and size. Even if I'd shouted Soli's name, I doubt whether he'd have responded.

I covered myself with Vaseline from the waist down and sun cream from the waist up, then put my helmet and gloves on. I was off at last.

It wasn't the most auspicious start; the gears on my bike appeared to have a mind of their own. Fortunately, one of the wizard mechanics was able to repair them, but this meant I was thirty minutes behind the other riders and once I set off again, I was pedalling like mad to try to make up the lost time and reach my cycling companions.

The temperature rose steadily to eighty degrees Fahrenheit. It was bad enough cycling, without those temperatures. By the time I got to the first 'pit stop' some of the riders were already leaving. The pit stop consisted of tables set up in the middle of nowhere, with bottles of water to drink and bags of nuts for energy. *Where were the tents for toilets?* No chance. The toilets were bushes or rocks with no toilet paper supplied! I must remember to take some in my carrier. So me, being me, walked off in another direction from everybody else to get some privacy. Never again!

After finding a suitable rock, I was just about to squat down when a snake swished through the sand. I ran back, well, more of a cross between the hurdles and a 100-metre race than a run, trying to pull my shorts up at the same time. I was close to being hysterical when I tried to tell the others about my experience. They said, "That's why everyone goes together, safety in numbers." By the end of our trip nobody bothered about that little thing called privacy.

Whilst on this ride, it had been arranged that I'd be wearing a microphone, so each morning, Steve, our sound- and cameraman, came around and fed a wire up my T-shirt. A pause for a few bleeped-out expletives (mine) and a microphone was clipped on to my collar. It could have been embarrassing, going to the loo and Steve being deafened, especially when the odd snake slithered past! Every time we stopped I had to remember to disconnect the thing.

The film crew travelled in a Land Rover that could go off-road. Initially I thought this would be great, because at least they'd be able to hear if I was in trouble, then I could just shout. Unfortunately, they could only pick me up if I was close by. I was determined that I would avoid trouble, if I could, when out of range.

The day didn't get any better. Half an hour after starting to ride again, one of the other girls got a little too close to me whilst going over some large rocks. She clipped my back wheel and I went over the handlebars. The bike fell on to my chest, with her sprawled on top of it. My leg and finger were cut. The handlebars left a dent in my sternum and bruising to my chest. I was really shaken up.

We had a doctor and mini bus travelling with us as part of our team, for just such emergencies. The doctor, known to us all as 'Dr Sophie', patched me up and suggested I didn't do the rest of the ride that day. There was no way I could fail. I knew I had to complete every single kilometre of the ride, so Dr Sophie gave me some painkillers and anti-inflammatories. I dusted myself off and got on the bike again.

The rest of the ride was terrible that day, so hard and uncomfortable. When my mentor, Julie, realised what had happened, she cycled with me to make sure I was OK and to give me her support. What a special lady she is.

I still felt so battered and bruised from the fall that it made me very emotional again. The accident had really thrown me, literally. My recent past caught up with me and it was difficult to focus on what I was doing there. My head just wasn't with me for a while as I pedalled more miles on automatic pilot. After a while and a lot of potholes later, I started to concentrate on the road again, and my mood lifted somewhat. It was a very wobbly moment for me, excuse the pun.

Eventually, we arrived at our first tent stop. The tents were erected by a team of wonderful locals who travelled before us every day on an open-top lorry, laden with Raj-style tents, truckle beds, Indian rugs, our luggage, and even china toilets.

By the time we arrived, the tents had been erected with two truckle beds put up in each one, Indian rugs laid out in the sand. Every tent had an improvised en-suite. This small room was reached through a flap at the back of the tent. The china toilet was placed over a hole in the ground, just placed, I might add, so it was extremely precarious. It was so important to sit on it squarely. There was also a bowl and jug to wash in. The shower was a water butt complete with jug and ladle. No mirrors. To flush the toilet, you just used a jug of water. Welcome to camping!

Our local guide was called 'The General'. Part fixer, part guru, he was an intuitive, wise and intelligent man who seemed to know exactly what was going on in your head before you even opened your mouth. What a character he was – his words and manner knowing exactly how to offer support or a hug where needed. I looked forward to the times we met up on the way.

The men would pile the holdalls for the ninety riders in a heap in the centre of the campsite. We'd have to find our own bag amongst them. Once located, we had to lug it back to our tent which might be quite some distance away. This is where I wished I'd cut down on my packing – that bag seemed to get heavier by the day.

Dr Sophie had her own tent and each night a queue would form outside. It was like a mini doctor's surgery. There were women with mostly nappy rash or something to do with that area, upset stomachs, or like me just needing to be patched up again. At least none of us needed sleeping tablets after spending between ten to twelve hours in the saddle; I certainly slept soundly.

A team of cooks travelled with us, their lorry laden down with gas stoves, beautiful copper dishes, plates, cutlery, and food. Each meal time they set up in the middle of nowhere. There were trestle tables covered with white linen cloths, canopies to shade us from the midday sun, and Indian carpets to sit on. They served our food up in copper tureens. It was vegetarian, buffet-style food, obviously to lessen the chance of tummy upsets. The food that was cooked was mostly curry dishes: poppadums, naan bread, various types of rice, vegetable dishes, an Indian dessert, and something to drink was the standard fare. The men who served us wore white gloves. It looked delightful and very proper.

That first tent stop was in the grounds of a ladies' college near the village of Bhusawar and although I was still feeling terrible after my earlier tumble, I managed to get a quick wash and some food.

That night we were being entertained by the pupils of the school with a special show of Indian dancing. It was amazing to watch. By the end of the evening I was so stiff; every muscle in my body ached. I limped and hobbled my way back to the tent which I shared with my cycling partner, Susie.

I'd managed to get a miner's torch before I left the UK. It came in very handy, especially when trying to eat my dinner in the dark, walking through sand, or even going to the loo.

What a relief it was to lay my head down that night. It didn't matter that the bed was hard and uncomfortable; I cuddled into my sleeping bag, pulled the zip up, and, knowing we had to be up at 6.00am the next day, closed my eyes and slept.

I woke at about 5.45am, my first taste of trying to get washed and dressed in the dark, apart from the light from the miner's torch. No flushing loo and no privacy either. My emotions were so up and down yet again, my chest still hurt from the accident, and I felt frightened about what lay ahead of me that day.

Chapter 4 – Day Two

Bhusawar to Bhandrej
Monday, 20 November 2006

The next section of the ride was taking us from Bhusawar to Bhandrej, approximately ninety-nine kilometres. We were told that because of the terrain it was probably equivalent to one hundred and forty kilometres in Britain.

We started on the main Agra–Jaipur highway, which was very busy. There were buses jammed with people, not only inside, but sitting on the roof and hanging out of side windows. There were motor bikes with animals and everything but the kitchen sink piled on them. How they stayed up I just don't know. No crash helmets!

The dust was awful. It filled our noses and mouths as vehicles passed. What humbles me, speaking as a moderately proficient cyclist now, is the skill with which the Indians continue to pedal their bicycles through these overcrowded areas, with staggering amounts of luggage and goods attached not just to their bicycles but to themselves as well. Each rider looked as though a puff of wind would knock him off his bike, yet he was able to keep upright and mobile. Amazing.

The next part of the day was quieter; on the secondary roads there were potholes and stretches without tarmac: Rajasthan rural life at its best and worst.

The countryside was beautiful but some of the rural villages we passed through were awful; raw sewage – which we nicknamed 'soup' – ran through the centre of the streets. It was very easy to fall into it; in fact, one girl did and ended up in hospital. The streets were so uneven under the 'soup'. If you slowed down too much you were likely to hit a boulder and come off. The smell was awful and during these times the only way I could stop myself from being sick was to pull up the sweat scarf I wore around my neck to cover my mouth and nose. I remember inhaling the faint aroma of linen that still lingered on the scarf.

We had several security men travelling with us: they'd do a quick recce before we cycled through the rural villages, but with the number of women cycling, it was almost impossible for them to be everywhere. We did our best to respect the Indian culture, wearing capped sleeved T-shirts and long cycling shorts. Local women from Rajasthan didn't ride bicycles, so we were seen almost as 'loose women' and were therefore harassed by local men or sometimes by the older women. Some of the locals even swung half-inch camel thorns on stems as we passed. If they caught you, they'd leave a very nasty scratch. One of our ladies had a stone thrown at her. I had my bottom pinched and breast touched by a local man, and was spat at by an elderly woman. Some locals laid thorns on the road, but these incidents were few. The majority of them welcomed us, waving and clapping as we passed. There were some sensitive areas we had to pass through, so the security team travelling with us was upped from fifty to sometimes a hundred men.

There was so much poverty. I spent a lot of time getting very distressed at the conditions people lived in. There were newborn babies wrapped in sacking, children with distorted limbs from poor nutrition, and so many beggars. In the midst of all this apparent poverty and need, I could see links to my own past – not the poverty and filth – but how wonderful it was to be able to see villages thronging with people, all chatting and laughing. The children played games in groups, as we did when we were young. Where could you see that now in England? The only time you seem to meet people is at work, in the supermarket, or at social functions. Children are often locked away in their sterile homes and small gardens. Excitement is a games console in their bedroom. What has happened to personal interaction? It's such a shame. These children in India were alive, vibrant, sociable, happy, independent, and totally at one with their surroundings. I learnt so much from that. I felt sad for their lot, but they seemed happy. There's much to be said for that.

That day was an incredibly hard ride. We reached our next overnight stop, Bhandrej Village, where we were spending the night in Bhadrawati Palace Hotel. It was beautiful, built around the eleventh century, and converted to a hotel in 1994. The plumbing was not the best. Water trickled out of the taps. It was an odd brown colour and after it had finished trickling for a few minutes, it stopped. I tried to have a bath and wash my hair but realised it could take all night to get a few inches of water.

I was so exhausted but, worst of all, had no feeling in my right hand. It was completely numb. I thought I was having a stroke, so off I went to see Dr Sophie. She carried out a few physical tests and assured me that it wasn't a stroke; it was the ulna nerve in my wrist and quite common on a ride like this. She said it was caused by the pressure of holding the handlebars tight when going over all those bumps. The feeling in that hand didn't return completely for about six weeks.

The mechanics fixed approximately eighty to one hundred punctures that day. Luckily, my bike didn't have one of them. I'm not sure I could have coped with that as well.

The next day's ride sounded even harder. The briefing that night informed us we would be cycling approximately seventy-seven kilometres, starting with some short off-road sections through dry river beds. I thought we'd already done that! We'd then cycle to the seven-hundred-year-old Abhaneri ancient temple complex, and the roads would become rougher and narrower as the day went on.

Later, we'd be cycling through more arid and hillier countryside, then camping on the edge of the Sariska Tiger Park. *Who am I kidding when I say I can do this?* With no feeling in my bum or right hand, I just wanted to cry, go back to England, and eat anything but curry.

I've never been one to daydream, but during those long hours in the saddle I often found myself drifting away, not to other places but with thoughts and ideas. It was quite distracting really, just something small would set me off – a smell or sight or even a fleeting cloud – and suddenly I'd be away in the mystical depths of my brain. I was discovering that I have far more imagination than I had realised before. Being out of my comfort zone and the organised life that I'd been used to was freeing up my mind and I was impressed by some of the thoughts I had. This country evokes a lot of musings about evolution and what was happening in the world. In the West, technology was king. Here, life was important. What appears to be so awful to people in the developed world are just acts of God in the Third World. Do they have insurance cover? I don't think so. I pedalled on.

Chapter 5 – Day Three

Bhandrej to Tehla Campsite
Tuesday, 21 November 2006

The next morning, we were up before 6am as Susie had been violently sick for a good hour and a few of the other cyclists had come down with it too. To Susie's horror, she was told she'd have to travel in the bus and rest. Poor girl, she wanted to do every single kilometre and felt she'd failed. She did try two kilometres, but had to give up. After tackling this particular day's ride, I wished I'd been on the bus!

It was a hell of a day. As the briefing had told us, the terrain was awful. We went through a dry river bed, lots of soft sand, and the roads were really bad. One of the professional riders travelling with us said the five kilometres travelled on one road was probably one of the worst roads in India. What? Then the route went up a mountain! Someone had told me there were no real hills on this ride.

I zigzagged up to the top of one, feeling good that I'd managed the climb, only to be chased by monkeys. It was a hoard, a swarm, a scream – a lot, to say the least. I knew that monkeys in the area carried rabies, so I got a move on.

It was a bad day. Restless natives spat at me, and while I was waiting for the mechanics to come to fix my puncture, two young Indian men on a moped stopped to ask if I wanted sex. I pretended to fiddle with my bike for fifteen minutes whilst they were there, trying not to give them any eye contact. Sex! I had no feeling from the waist down! Joking apart, it was very frightening.

Usually, for safety, if any of us had a puncture the next cyclist coming past waited with you until the mechanics arrived, but unfortunately that day there was nobody around. It was so strange, being in the middle of rural India, where none of the local population spoke English, yet these two young men knew how to ask for sex? It must be a universal language.

I completed a long section of off-road cycling, and then climbed a narrow path uphill. As I rounded a bend at the summit, the film crew were there waiting for me. I was out of breath, tired, and as I passed they asked me how I was. To this, I raised my numb hand, and replied with a gesture and swear word, which I'm not going to repeat. This was shown on the programme with a bleep in place of the word. If I'd got off the bike I'd probably have chucked it at them. They caught me at a bad moment. The footage was later shown on *This Morning*. Fern commented, "What happened to the nice, polite Jill?" I knew the day wasn't Friday the 13th but boy it really did feel like it.

This cycle ride wasn't just a physical thing; it was a mental challenge as well. Even though most of the time there were other people around, I was incredibly lonely. I didn't know anyone on a personal level so couldn't open up to them about how I was feeling. I was still trying to be a smiley person, all things to all people, and it was becoming much harder. I wanted to scream, swear, cry, and die: my comfy little world was in danger of falling down. The purpose of this challenge was to find the real me, but was the real me a gibbering wreck? I wanted to get to safety, lock all the doors, and never come out again. If this is facing up to myself, forget it. I'd rather be who I was, smiley Jill. These negative thoughts weren't doing me any favours. I forced myself to think of something positive, no matter how small, such as how many hours it was until bedtime.

The day carried on getting worse. We were just two kilometres away from our next campsite, and I had yet another puncture. Dusk was falling, and I was very scared. There were lots of unfriendly villagers around including children, one of whom pinched the water bottle from my bike. With my experiences earlier in the day I was feeling very vulnerable. Some of the other riders caught up with me, and realised I was in a bit of a state. I was determined to ride that bike, puncture and all, to our next stop. If I'd waited, a van would have picked me up as we weren't allowed to ride once it was dark. This group of riders cocooned me, singing, talking, and most of all staying with me until we reached the camp. What a wonderful group of women – and how I needed them at that moment.

On arriving at the campsite, I was so exhausted and stiff I couldn't even raise my leg to get off the bike, or, as the girls commented, I was, "Unable to get my leg over." All I wanted was a hot bubble bath, some fluffy towels, a nice cup of tea, and cheese on toast, as well as a soft armchair to curl up in. That night we had a buffet of, yes, curry. Under any other circumstances I'd have loved a curry, but for the past few days it was all we'd eaten for breakfast, lunch, and dinner. I wanted something without spice in it. Even the cold porridge I'd had on my first morning seemed a better option.

After realising how tired I was, I decided on an early night and made my way back to the tent, which I was sharing with Susie. I found it very difficult to walk in the dark across the soft sand with only the miner's torch to guide my way. As normal, everything had been set up before we'd arrived that day – twin beds erected, Indian rug laid on the soft sand, the toilet precariously sitting over a hole made in the ground, and a stand for the bowl and jug. On arriving at the tent, I noticed that a couple of the door ties were undone. I felt sure they were all secured before we'd left for our evening meal. As I was on my own, I very hesitantly entered the tent. I immediately noticed lots of silver paper scattered everywhere, which I later discovered was from a secret stash of chocolate that Susie had packed in her holdall. Therefore, assuming a jackal had got into the tent and not sure if it was still around, I ran back to find one of the sound crew. I shouted, "There's a Jekyll in my tent!" The reply I got was, "Where's Mr Hyde?" They came back with me to check the tent out, but there was only a pile of chocolate papers to be seen. I didn't live that one down for quite a while.

By this time, I wasn't only tired but worried that something might enter our tent during the night. After managing to fix the ties as best I could, I retired for the night, my sleeping bag zip done up so tightly I could hardly breathe. No Jekylls, please.

Chapter 6 – Day Four

Tehla Camp to Doela Campsite
Wednesday, 22 November 2006

We rose the next morning at 6am; this was to be our fourth day of riding. I still felt tired and stiff. I was having serious doubts as to whether or not I could do it any more. The day before had just about killed me. I wanted to stop and rest, but after popping a couple of anti-inflammatory tablets I felt a little better. At this stage, I was prepared to do just about anything to get myself through it. If someone had offered me illegal drugs, I'm sure I'd have been tempted to take them. Having always been the kind of person who was very controlled, this would never have crossed my mind in the past. Even drinking too much, and certainly the idea of taking something illegal, wouldn't have occurred to me. If that happened, I'd be out of control. The idea of taking anything apart from a few anti-inflammatory tablets showed just how low I'd got.

We'd been informed the previous night that the next stage of the ride would be approximately ninety-eight kilometres. The terrain would be less exotic and more arid. We were to stop en route and visit the ruins of an ancient city, which was reached by cycling on the edge of the Sariska National Park, where there was a good chance we'd see some wildlife. I'd seen all the wildlife I wanted to see. What was the wildlife anyway? The odd tiger, maybe? We were warned that parts of the roads would be in bad condition. Bad condition wasn't the phrase I'd have used!

The campsite we were staying at transpired to be one of the most spectacular sites of the trip; our tents nestled between white sand dunes, near to the village of Doela, with views of two ancient forts on hills in the background.

The first stage of the ride wasn't too bad, but by the second stage the temperature was in the eighties, with very little shelter from trees as we were cycling across desert, then up those 'non-existent' hills. Fern was known for always having a large pot of Vaseline with her, so often when we were uncomfortable we would wave her down. This day she was stopped several times! By the time we reached our break stop, I felt very dehydrated even though I had a back pack filled with water, known as a 'Camel', which I was regularly drinking from through a tube clipped on to my shoulder strap. My head was throbbing and I felt completely out of it. After some energy drinks, nuts, and a banana I felt slightly human again. Applying yet another half jar of Vaseline from my thighs to my hips, sun cream to my face and arms, and two plasters to my right and left thumb to cover up the blisters that I'd gained off-road from hanging on to the bike for grim death, I was off again.

**

My mental health was now really starting to worry me – I wondered how many beetles and bugs I'd squashed during the ride. I felt like a cycling Attila the Hun. *Would I be written up in history as the woman responsible for the death and mutilation of a million bugs?* Legs like jelly, no sensation from the knees down, I wondered if my feet had welded themselves to the pedals. *How much longer to the campsite?* I was ravenous.

We passed through a village where the monkeys looked menacing and in attacking mood. I felt very frightened. The village looked like something from the film *Raiders of the Lost Ark*. It had ancient monuments and buildings, ivy growing out of crevices, and the odd bush appearing from stone pillars. Monkeys jumped in and out of the buildings. I often wondered why *This Morning* had given us bright yellow T-shirts to wear – it certainly seemed to attract the monkeys! The bonus was that the locals seemed friendlier. Children and elderly people welcomed us, smiling and waving as we passed. That couldn't be said of the monkeys.

A yellow-garbed holy man was sitting cross-legged by the side of the road with a wooden bowl by his side. He talked quietly to a number of people. How wonderful to have such faith, not having to rely on oneself but on a higher authority, an all-enveloping entity, just abide by the rules and you are safe; you don't have the control; someone or something else does. Maybe this would be a good life for me? But on the other hand, is it another form of submission? I don't know. What I do know is, if I couldn't pedal for another two hours, I'd miss the pit stop.

That day I only just managed to make it to the campsite, which was at the top of yet another very steep hill. It must have been at least a one-in-three! The heat was incredible, even though it was late afternoon. I really thought I was going to collapse. Someone had to help me off the bike, everyone being supportive and having a bit of a laugh as I tried to dismount. In the end they laid my bike on its side, to enable me to get off. I thought that I'd never be able to move again. Please someone, give me a comfy bed, but most of all a hot bath. The sand and dirt in my hair was making my head itch. I so wanted to wash my hair. I fantasised about a plate of fish and chips drenched in salt and vinegar. My mouth watered at the idea.

The good thing was that we arrived in the light. I suppose it could have been worse – at least I didn't have to pitch the tent. After dragging my holdall to my lodgings, a quick wash with cold water, and a brief rest for fifteen minutes, I felt human again.

That night we were invited to watch an Indian cookery demonstration. On leaving the tent I was greeted by an amazing sunset. It was absolutely spectacular; the view from the campsite was wonderful. I'll always treasure that image. I made my way over to where the cookery demonstration was being held and I was treated to a rare glimpse of traditional Indian cuisine. Yes, I know it was curry but that night I really enjoyed it. It may have helped that I knew the next day was to be the last day of our ride and I thought, "Jill, you may actually finish this, notwithstanding the bloody curry!"

Chapter 7 – The end of the ride

Doela Camp to Jaipur
Thursday, 23 November 2006

Thursday dawned, the last day of the ride. We were allowed an extra half an hour's lie in, which meant not rising until 6.30am.

I started the day with mixed feelings. Whereas before I couldn't wait for this day to come, now I wasn't so sure. I wondered what would happen to me after the challenge was finished. It had been my life for the past few months – my main focus with the training, visits to ITV, radio interviews and newspaper reports. The team of people helping and supporting me had made me feel so special. *How would it be without this?* I decided that I needed to concentrate on that day's ride and not to worry about the next day until it arrived.

That day the ride was much shorter, only fifty-two kilometres. We'd cycle through an arid area that resembled a desert, starting on an undulating road between sand dunes. Next, there would be about five kilometres of dust track, which would take us through a river before joining a tarmac road again to Tehla. We were to complete the challenge at a place called Lal Mahal, where we would have lunch and then transfer to Jaipur overnight.

Breakfast was served at 7.00am with the sun rising over the campsite. Overnight, by way of a change, we'd had rain and thunder which apparently isn't unusual in the desert. By way of no change, we had curry!

We were on our bikes by 8.00am and cycled twenty-seven kilometres before our first stop. Everyone was on such a high, singing as we pedalled. Fern kept us going with her rendition of 'Singing in the Rain'. Twenty-seven kilometres seemed nothing that day. Then another eighteen kilometres, this time stopping at a stunning hotel. We had cold drinks and energy biscuits.

The highlight though was that the hotel had the luxury of a flushing loo. It had a lockable door, soap, running water, a towel, and a mirror, which I wish I hadn't looked into. I couldn't believe how excited I was to be able to sit on a toilet, complete with loo roll, instead of hovering behind a bush, over a hole in the ground, or sitting on a wobbly loo in the tent. It was clean and fresh. I wanted to stay there forever and admire that little room, watching clear water coming out of a tap. The hotel gardens were beautiful and overlooked a crocodile lake, but, thank goodness, there were no crocodiles as the lake had almost dried up.

We completed a further eight kilometres and re-grouped for the final one and a half kilometres. What a fantastic feeling as the *This Morning* team led all those women across the finishing line.

I'd actually done it. I had cycled every single kilometre. How I managed to complete this ride and where the strength came from I've still no idea, but I found it helped to take each bit of road as it came – and trying not to worry about what came next.

Still astride my bicycle, I collapsed over my handlebars. My feelings were again all over the place. I wanted to pinch myself and see if it was really me in that place at that time. There were waves of elation, joy, and sadness, crying so much I thought I'd burst. I said I'd do this and I'd carried it through.

Though I felt that huge sense of achievement, my mind began to think once again about what would happen after this adventure. So many people were celebrating around me, but a part of me inside felt a little lost and bewildered by it all. In some ways I still couldn't believe that I'd completed all these challenges in such a short time, and when people congratulated me, I almost wondered why.

The rest of that day was brilliant; we were all given a medal threaded on pink ribbon which we wore proudly around our necks, with a beautiful garland of sweet smelling flowers. There was entertainment, lashings of champagne, and a buffet lunch outside on the lawns of the beautiful Lal Mahal hotel. It seemed very strange to think our challenge was completed.

After several glasses of champagne and with our stomachs full we were bussed into Jaipur, which was one hour away. Everybody was booked into a hotel there. After days in tents and washing in buckets, that first shower was so wonderful. Clear warm water cascaded over my bruised and battered body. If someone else hadn't been waiting to use the shower after me, I could have stayed in there all day. Even after standing under it for ten minutes, sand and dust were still coming off me. The towel I dried myself on started off white but by the time I'd finished it was a funny shade of brown/grey. I did smell much better though.

That evening we were invited to a demonstration given by a local clothing company and shown how to tie saris. We had the opportunity to buy them afterwards. The art of wearing and tying these beautiful garments seemed very complicated but I was glad to learn a little about Indian culture. Then it was dinner and bed.

After breakfast the next day our suitcases were loaded on to a van for their journey back to New Delhi. We were taken by bus for a tour around the Amber Fort, which was amazing, then the rest of the day around Jaipur, generally known as the Pink City due to the distinctive salmon-coloured facades of its older buildings.

During the afternoon, the *This Morning* team took me to a location overlooking a place called *Palace of Water* for my last interview. What a wonderful setting. I felt so emotional reflecting on all that had happened over the past few days.

I recounted the accident on my first day and the puncture two kilometres from the campsite on day three. I spoke about the fact I'd been taken to my extreme limit and felt so vulnerable and needy – in fact, how I'd felt most of my life.

I told of how Julie Dawn Cole, my fitness coach, and now friend, had given me the support I needed and said she'd ride with me after the accident, and how I'd realised after that day that I'd turned a corner and felt I was going to be OK.

Starting to integrate, talking and riding with the other women, and hearing their stories helped me enormously. They were such a wonderful bunch.

Seeing the monkeys, the raw sewage running through the villages, the small baby wrapped in an old potato sack for protection, and the locals spitting and grabbing me, I thought how my life would change as a consequence of this journey.

When the interview was concluded, we all had lunch. Then we met with our guide – 'The General'. At the end of our trip he asked me to contact him, saying I'd benefit from a walk across the Himalayas. I may just do that one day.

During the afternoon the General accompanied us to the local markets of Jaipur. He was useful to have around as he negotiated and bartered with the local traders, which enabled us to benefit from great discounts on all our gifts to take home. I discovered a little shop that sold 'Pringles' and thought "great – plain crisps, no spice!" Unfortunately, on opening them they were curry flavoured. I didn't eat them.

Chapter 8 – Trains and planes

We boarded the coach back to the hotel to pick up our hand luggage and a short while later we were heading to Jaipur railway station. What a place that was – I've never seen so many people. It seemed even busier than Paddington Station at peak times. We were warned about pickpockets. That didn't surprise me, considering the number of people around. The five-hour journey from Jaipur to New Delhi was due to start at around 6pm. It was quite an experience. As our train pulled in, I thought it resembled my brother's trainset when he was a young boy – an engine pulling little wooden boxes. At least it was good value, costing approximately £7 including snacks.

The carriages were packed with passengers. It was so noisy, with everybody speaking in different languages. An Indian man came around with trays of food containing samosa, a sandwich with egg and something unidentifiable, two chocolate éclair sweets, a carton of juice which was four months out of date, and some sachets of tea and sugar. I was extremely careful about what I ate of that little lot. The sandwich and orange juice didn't appeal. I managed the sweets and tea, without milk though.

The journey proceeded well until an insect about four inches long came through one of the open windows. Goodness knows what it was. It resembled a caterpillar, except much heavier. That was when it became obvious who wasn't local on that train. All the British people let out a yell; some of the girls I was travelling with even stood on their seats. Not me though, I just gripped the arm of the person sitting next to me! The locals appeared to know what it was and didn't seem at all fazed. They just waved it away.

We were due to arrive at New Delhi railway station about 10.20pm. By 9.00pm I was bursting for the loo, but knew from other people's reaction after visiting it that it wasn't a pleasant experience. My bladder had felt full for at least an hour and I'd put off going, but couldn't wait any longer. There was no lock on the door, so one of the group who'd already experienced the delight said it wasn't so bad and offered to hold the door closed for me. I went in, and then tried to escape straight away, but the door was held firmly, and I was told "just go". The smell was suffocating; I tried not to breathe, but eventually had to. The toilet was just a hole going straight through to the railway track. We were travelling at some speed; bits of twig and debris were being sucked up through the hole, which was caked in excrement. As I hovered over it, to answer the call of nature, I hadn't allowed for the air coming up from the ground. It was like a Yellowstone geyser: I was soaked by my own urine. I really wished I'd studied physics at school, I'd have known about updraught. I still live with the horror of the thought of needing a number two rather than just emptying my bladder. I'd have hated to sit in that all the way to Delhi! I now understand why the local population wear loose clothing; at least they can pull it up around their necks – a bit more difficult with a pair of Levis!

It was past midnight when we pulled into New Delhi station, but surprisingly there were still so many people around. The pavements outside were covered by a multitude of slumbering people; it looked as if every space was filled. People on their own, and sometimes whole families, adults and several children all sleeping huddled under blankets. I wondered whether they were just travelling and breaking their journeys or were they homeless and that's how life is for them. Everything around them was very tidy; I even saw one man with a large palm leaf, sweeping around the area he was about to lie down on. How sad it was to see so many people sleeping like that, bodies lying straight on to concrete, no mattress or padding, and all their worldly goods packed around them.

I'd fantasised all through the journey, thinking I would

sleep in a proper bed and have another lovely shower. When we reached the hotel at past 1.00am, everybody got a real shock. What a terrible place. It was more like a hovel. Really filthy: wallpaper peeling off the walls, the beds with grimy sheets which looked alive and jumping – I wouldn't have even felt happy in a sleeping bag, let alone sleeping in them. The mattresses were hard as well. My skin crawled. There was an en-suite facility, but on entering I couldn't believe the state it was in. Black mouldy shower curtain, the wash basin, bath, and toilet black with grime. The toilet looked very similar to the one on the train. The door to our room had a lock on it, but the edges looked as if someone had tried to force it open with a crowbar. The only thing I'd say in favour of the room was that it would be a great backdrop for some seedy film.

An experience of a lifetime was to finish like this. Please, please, it can't happen. It just can't, it wasn't fair. Then Susie, who I was sharing with, came up from reception saying Fern would definitely not stay there and wouldn't allow us to either, after what we'd achieved, so we packed again. Some of the things I'd taken out of my holdall had already been put straight back in because I was so worried about what 'wildlife' my belongings may have picked up in the room. We joined Fern downstairs. By this time it was 2.00am. Fern had arranged for one of the film crew to drive us to the 'Oberoi Hotel' in New Delhi. If it had been scored in cricket terms, this was a six! It was an oasis in the middle of the city.

We pulled up outside this magnificent hotel. The doorman, complete with gold and white robes and matching turban, opened the doors for us. He put our entire luggage on a trolley and wheeled it into reception. Wow! It was so grand – ornate ceilings and pillars, the smell of orchids and lilies, fresh fruit by the basketful. Apparently, the Oberoi is one of the most exclusive hotels in the capital of India and overlooks the prestigious New Delhi Golf Club. It has an aquamarine pool, several restaurants, international boutiques, spa, and fitness centre.

Fern signed us in. What an amazing, caring woman she is, paying for our stay out of her own pocket. I had my own room – well, more like two or three standard hotel rooms rolled into one. It was fantastic. A queen size bed, piled high with cushions, with a note on the pillow which read, "If this pillow isn't correct for you, we will change it for the right one". It felt incredible after spending days cycling – a huge room, desk, fresh roses, chocolates, and fresh fruit. I hadn't eaten fresh fruit since my arrival in India. The bathroom was such a delight; I discovered a soft white bath robe and slippers, white fluffy towels, and Molton Brown products to bathe and shower in. It was heaven.

Fern had invited us for drinks in her room. I dropped my hand luggage off and went along. On arriving, her door was unlocked. She called out from the bathroom to come in and make ourselves at home. She was already in the bath, soaking in a mass of perfumed bubbles. She just couldn't wait. Drinks and nibbles arrived. After a chat, a few glasses of something appropriate and with the clock's hands at 4.00am, I went back to my room. I filled the bath with water and bubbles, showering first to remove yet more sand from my hair. After a blissful soak, I snuggled down into the most comfortable bed I'd ever had and slept soundly until mid-morning.

Breakfast was served in my room. What a delight. Hot porridge, milk and sugar, served on beautiful bone china, followed by poached eggs, wholemeal bread, and tea. I ate it so quickly I thought I was going to be sick. I was so hungry.

Later that day we went for a browse around the local market, followed by a tour of the famous Red Fort. That evening we were to celebrate our achievements with a Gala Dinner, which was to be held in a beautiful park near to our hotel.

I packed my case for the last time, then got ready for the evening ahead. Wow, how nice was this, my own bathroom and being able to get ready in proper light, no miner's lamp. Being able to see what I was doing was a real treat. I dressed in my Indian outfit and pashmina purchased at the market that day.

As the dinner was held outside, once the sun went down it became rather cold. I was very pleased I had my newly acquired pashmina. I needed it.

What a celebration we had that night! Everybody was on a high from completing the ride and knowing that we would be flying home the next day. We had the most wonderful buffet, Indian food, but the best yet. It was rather strange; I was unable to recognise anybody. They looked completely different with their hair washed, make-up applied, and wearing colourful saris or Indian attire. Not one piece of mud or cycling gear was to be seen anywhere. After several pictures were taken, we had a recital of the poem that Julie Dawn Cole composed with the help of several members of the *This Morning* team. It says it all rather well.

Cycle India 2006

There were 100 women on wheels
Who ate nothing but curry for meals
Undulations they travelled
As their bums came unravelled
And the locals all copped a good feel.

The monkeys all laughed
As the ladies rode past
Puffing and panting up hills.
Though quickly they scattered
'Cos the girls were all knackered
But it's amazing what you can do
With a few pills!

They camped out at night
And looked quite a sight
In their Lycra and sweat-stained attire.
But a bucket of water
Just aimed where it ought to
Was able to put out the fire.

A rumour was heard
Now this may sound absurd
That a 'Jekyll' was running amok.
He's stolen some choccy
In fact the whole blokkie
And gobbled the whole bleeding lot!

They cycled in pain
And drove Yochi insane
With the number of punctures they had
But after 250 he became quite nifty
For the use of his tool they were glad.

As they tumbled and crashed
And their bodies were smashed
Doctor Sophie came into her own.
She cleaned and she squirted
And patched where it hurted
And never was she heard to moan.

We cycled through soup
And some of the group
Decided to go in for a dip.
It didn't taste great
And they just couldn't wait
To get back to camp and just strip.

Saddle sore and weary
And often quite teary
They pedalled because they must
Past peacocks and pigs
Even camels with wigs
And all they could see was … dust!

For the ladies to pee
Where the whole world could see
Was really quite an art
They had to find bushes
For those little white tushies
As they tried really hard not to … Wince!

The last day was here
And with a very sore rear
We approached our dear old machines
With pure determination
We'd conquered that nation
Fuelled on dahl and baked beans!

With sadness it ends
So goodbye to new friends
It's time for us all to go home.
And aren't we all glad
We're a little bit mad?
But next year I'm going to Rome!

A couple of songs and more drinks, then we returned to our wonderful hotel where even more drinks were on offer. Such a lovely conclusion to our journey and it was all down to Fern.

The next morning it was back to an early start again, 7.00am to be exact. A forty-five-minute trip to New Delhi Airport for our nine-hour journey back to the UK. It looked as if we would be travelling economy class on our return journey, but at the last minute we were upgraded to upper class again. It was comfy seats, Buck's Fizz, free bar, and films all the way home. Wow, how the other half live. I wondered if I'd ever travel like that again.

As we landed, I felt very emotional. Everybody had their husbands, partners, or families meeting them. There was nobody waiting for me, except the chauffeur to drive me back to Wiltshire. My head was full of thoughts of what my life would be like now. This all had been such a huge part of it for the past few months. *What would the future hold for me?*

As I said a sad goodbye to Fern, Julie, and all the team, I couldn't help wondering what was to become of me. I walked towards the barrier, everyone so pleased to see their families, and there was my chauffeur with his card held high with my name on. I knew him as he'd picked me up on several occasions at the ITV studios. He seemed so pleased to see me; it was almost as if he knew how difficult this part was. He said he and his wife had kept up to date with our progress and told me how well I'd done.

As my journey 'home' continued he asked if I was hungry, which I was, so we stopped at the first services where he kindly treated me to a Chicken Royale, chips and a cup of tea, saying it was the least he could do after what I'd been through. What a lovely man. I arrived back at my brother's house late that evening and, after talking about my experiences over a cup of tea, retired to bed exhausted and much deflated. A sense of anti-climax was setting in.

These recollections of my journey across that part of India are written very much as they came to mind, with vivid memories that will never leave me. Most are relayed from entries in my diary, written during those eleven days of being in a far-off land, on a bicycle at the age of fifty-six, away from the comforts of life, wondering what the heck I was doing there.

During my preparation for this journey, several people

suggested that I should write about my life and what I had achieved by putting my mind to it. I too felt that I had to write my story; I just had to. Not for others, but for me. I needed to show myself how far I'd come, since that first dark day when I knew that my marriage was over, and nothing would be the same again. Those eleven days in India started me thinking back to my beginnings and my earliest memories, and this helped me work out how and why I'd come to be where I was.

PART TWO

HOW IT ALL BEGAN

Chapter 9 – My background

I was one of three children, with an older sister and younger brother. My father was in the RAF. My mother was a trained seamstress and extremely good at her job. She was such a caring person, not just to her family, but to the community too.

Dad ruled the house like a sergeant major. I felt he was a bit of a tyrant. He was strict with us girls, but my brother seemed to get away with murder. My father appeared to dote on him. Even when the grandchildren arrived, he treated the grandsons differently from his granddaughters; he seemed to direct his attention to them, whereas the girls didn't seem quite so important.

My mother was always working hard and seemed so weary. The only affection I ever saw my father show towards her seemed to be when friends stayed: it almost seemed as if an act was put on for their benefit. I recognise her in myself, especially the way I was in my marriage – busy, busy, busy. My impression was that Dad didn't appear to treat her particularly well. She always seemed a little frightened of saying or doing the wrong thing and upsetting him. She never seemed that relaxed when he was around. Although he was a fairly short and lightly built man, you wouldn't want to cross him and invoke his wrath.

I often pondered whether this pattern of behaviour by my father was one of the reasons my mother was so happy helping other people. Perhaps her generosity of spirit was a substitute for the love and affection that may have been lacking in her own relationship. I wondered at times how she stayed in the marriage. Maybe by caring for others she got the fulfilment needed to survive? Her way of achieving some form of self-worth, being wanted and loved?

My father set out tasks for us to complete each week before we got our pocket money. Cleaning our rooms on a Saturday or changing our beds, complete with hospital corners. On Sundays, we cleaned the brass and polished floors, and when the chores were completed he would inspect our work.

Although I can remember some good times whilst growing up, my memories are mostly of the bad times. My relationship with Dad was volatile and it was always a struggle with constant battles between us. As a child, it always felt as though he didn't like me very much. I was never good enough: whatever I did, no matter how hard I tried, he never praised me for my efforts. This resulted in me becoming quite rebellious. Once I cut the whiskers off the cat just so I could gain attention. Even if the attention I received was negative, a slap or sent to my bedroom without tea, it was better than none at all. My mother always sneaked upstairs with a drink and food for me later.

With Dad being in the RAF, it meant that we didn't stay in one place for very long and lived in accommodation attached to the base where Dad happened to be posted, including two and a half years in Singapore.

After Singapore, we moved to the West Country and he was allocated a house about five miles from the base, an older pre-war, semi-detached, with good sized gardens front and back. He was a trained metalwork instructor and made double wrought iron gates for the drive entrance. The house had a small kitchen, sitting room, dining room, and three bedrooms. It was a pretty standard house of its time, but I don't remember it as being anything more than that. Certainly, I couldn't really describe it as 'home'. It was just somewhere in which we lived. Until I had my own house years later and put down my own roots, I didn't find that feeling. It must have been all the moving around.

I do have some happy memories. I was about ten when Dad bought a second-hand motorbike and sidecar which he was able to put us three children in and Mum on the pillion seat of the bike. Not only that, he also put a small boat, complete with oars, upside down on the roof of the sidecar. Then, off we'd all go to the river Avon and enjoy messing about on the boat. Mum even carried on doing her knitting sitting on the back of that bike.

After that he bought a car – a 'Bond Convertible' gold-coloured three-wheeler. It had no reverse gears. If Dad needed to reverse, we all had to pile out and physically pick it up and turn it in the opposite direction. He took us on day trips to the seaside and for outings locally.

Dad made us wooden stilts and lots of toffee apples. He would chop slivers of wood for the sticks and then make the toffee so hard and sticky that we nearly broke our teeth on it. Sometimes, he made chips for us and put them in a triangle of greaseproof paper with salt and vinegar, wrapped in newspaper.

For a while he had a van and he would bundle us children into the back of it to go and get fish and chips. The van was full of all sorts, from plastic guttering to lengths of copper piping, tools, and general paraphernalia. We sat on the floor – no seats, no seat belts, just us. The stuff slid everywhere as Dad drove around the corners. Going over the humpback bridge, Dad didn't slow up and everything in the back, including us, took off and clattered back to the floor. As we approached the bridge, he would tell us to say hello to the fairies as we flew. He would have to brake hard to get around the next corner, so we would end up squashed against the front seats with bits of everything bumping into us. We loved it.

Dad didn't seem to be afraid of anything. Even as an old man, I remember he would take his van down to the local bank where there would be no parking spaces, so he would abandon it in the middle of the road or park on double yellow lines. Traffic wardens would threaten him but to no avail, he still continued with this behaviour. Eventually, even they gave up on him.

When my father was dying from cancer he stayed with my sister for five months and I stayed with them for his final few weeks. I was in my late forties. During that time, we found out a little bit about his background, though Dad was very reluctant about discussing his upbringing.

His mother was a powerful woman, his father a bit of a mouse by all accounts. In fact, his mother had someone lined up for my father to marry, but Dad wasn't having any of that. He married his own choice, the girl who lived next door, which was unfortunate as the two families didn't get on well.

His mother had said, "If you marry her we will have nothing to do with you." None of his family attended their wedding and he saw very little of them after that. They were never mentioned whilst we grew up, apart from the fact that he had five sisters and he was the only boy. His mother seemed to resent him for some reason. He did everything for his sisters and mother, with very little praise.

He told us there were opportunities that came into his life which she prevented him from accepting, so I suppose at last I could understand why my Dad was the way he was. My sister and I always hoped that he would say that he loved us, if only just once, but he never did, even towards the end of his life.

This has been a sad chapter to write as I've tried to balance how I see my past and not to ignore the side of my father that could be so loving and caring. To try to understand why he was as he was, and how he coped with life and responsibilities through my childhood and up to the time of my marriage, is now much easier for me to see after all the years that have passed.

I now know that he tried to be a good father, but it had to be within his own parameters from his upbringing, and they weren't the best. I'm sorry to say that it was the overall coldness and distance in his character which is my lasting impression. Maybe he felt the same about his parents but couldn't alter himself and adjust to his own family. That's so sad.

On reflection, I do feel strongly my life could have been so much better if Dad had come to terms with, and made sense of, his own childhood. Perhaps he couldn't face his past and work out how to deal with it, although it was obvious he was very much affected by it.

Our past can shape us, our personalities, our emotions, our fears, our relationships, and how we want to lead our lives – or don't. However, I now know that my past does not control my future – only the choices I make *now* do that. Therefore I can choose to shape my own future. I can choose not to let the past govern the present. It's good to take stock, but it's never too late to forgive, and move on. While you have breath, it's never too late to tell someone you love them.

Chapter 10 – Always a worker

As children we were encouraged to earn our pocket money, and from the time it was legal for me to work, I did. My first job was two paper rounds, one before going to school and the other on Sundays, which my brother and I shared due to the larger area covered. My father made us a barrow as the Sunday papers were always much heavier. Christmas was the best time as our customers left tips. People were generous.

Whilst still at school I had several part-time jobs. My first was working in a wonderful little cake shop at weekends and during school holidays. That was great in the winter, with comforting smells of warm bread, spicy cakes, and gingerbread. Come summer it was a nightmare; I was stung so many times by wasps that had nestled into the cream buns.

At fifteen, I found a dream job at the *Three Gables* sweet shop in my local town. It was a proper sweet shop with shelves full of screw-top jars containing a huge array of sweets and on the counter in front of the till was the 'Pick and Mix'.

I have such a sweet tooth. The boss was rarely there, so I was able to dip freely into the jars of assorted sweets and often did. I placated my conscience by telling myself that it was one of the perks of the job.

The *Three Gables* has lived in my memory so vividly. Many years have passed since I worked there, but if I close my eyes I can be transported back to standing behind that counter. My boss allowed us to split packs of cigarettes and sell them in fives, therefore becoming a huge attraction to the older school children.

It was whilst working there that I met my husband-to-be. He attended a school nearby and came in with his mates to buy cigarettes. He made several visits to that little shop over the next few weeks, but I had no idea he was interested in me. He played guitar in a local pop group so he got a friend of his to deliver a note to me inviting me to a practice session, and that is how we started going out with each other. I became his girlfriend at the tender age of sixteen, with the added bonus of being able to go to their gigs, usually every two weeks. They were a very good band.

After leaving school my first job was working as a dental nurse and receptionist. My employer was a part-time dentist, part-time farmer. I know he was a very good farmer; I'm still not convinced about the dentist part. He was in his late sixties, a tall muscular man with hands that would deliver a calf with ease. He had the most amazing thick silver hair, reddish cheeks, and huge bright blue eyes. He was a really happy man but tight-fisted when it came to money, paying me a mere five pounds and ten shillings for a full week's work, of which I handed over two pounds and ten shillings to my father for housekeeping. After a few months of working there my father told me to ask for a pay rise, which I did. I got a whole five shillings.

The dental surgery itself was very old fashioned, complete with a non-electric drill which was driven by a foot pedal. If the dentist got involved in a conversation (albeit a one-sided one) with the patient, then his foot would get slower and slower on the pedal causing the patient to go rigid. I would notice their finger nails implanted deep into the soft leather arms of the chair. He would then ask the patient if it was hurting. The black leather dental chair, complete with nail marks in the arms, was a scary looking thing. It had a rolled leather adjustable head rest with a foot pedal at the side to adjust the height – all it needed was neck and arm straps with electrodes attached. It really did look like something out of a horror movie. No wonder I hate going to the dentist now!

After a year with the dentist I decided I would like to go to college and take two courses in catering, the initial one to qualify as a cook and the second in catering management. During my three years at college, I remember going home one day ecstatic after receiving 'The Best Student of the Year' award. I was presented with a book for my efforts. All I got from Dad when I told him was some sarcastic remark, whereas Mum gave me a huge hug and a kiss.

Chapter 11 – Marriage

After I graduated from college, having known my husband-to-be for four years, we decided to get married. He was twenty-one and I was twenty. He was in his final year at university. I was still a virgin, due to both my beliefs and my father's strict upbringing. Even after we were engaged if I ever arrived home not wearing my lipstick and was just ten minutes past my curfew time my father would ban me from going out for a week or two. It was made very obvious that my father didn't agree with my choice of partner. I did wonder if he would ever approve of anybody.

We had a big white wedding in our local church followed by a reception in a nearby pub's skittle alley, which I paid for. The buffet, if you can call it that, consisted of one sausage roll, a round of sandwiches, and a glass of sherry on arrival. This all for the princely sum of ten shillings per head.

Part of my catering training involved a course in patisserie, so I decided to save money and make the wedding cake myself. As it was my very first it wasn't the best: a two-tier fruit cake covered in royal icing, adorned with silver leaves and silk flowers. The worst part was the cake stood on pillars and I hadn't yet mastered the art of creating a flat cake. The finished ensemble on the top table ended up looking like the Leaning Tower of Pisa.

We couldn't afford a honeymoon, so after our reception we stopped at a pub for a slap-up dinner of steak and chips with a glass of red wine. Then on to our new home – a bedsit we were renting in Ely, near Cardiff University, where my husband was a student. The first floor flat consisted of one L-shaped room with a small kitchenette and bathroom. The bed was covered in bright orange nylon sheets and matching candlewick bedspread. How 60s was that? The furniture was a bit of an eclectic mix with a small flap-top second-hand table, two very battered dining chairs, and two old armchairs with small tables you could pull out, hidden in the arms. In the kitchenette we had a cooker and electric spin dryer which were given to us as wedding presents.

I've agonised over what, and indeed whether, to write about the intimate side of my married life and how it affected me. *Should I be open about my feelings – past and present? Could this part of my life be spoken about? Should it remain private?* I find it difficult to understand why some people feel free to discuss the sexual side of their relationships so openly when I think this is extremely personal and private. Yet despite having this viewpoint, I still want, and perhaps need, to say something.

These days, it's now almost impossible to get beyond the early teens without a comprehensive knowledge of what makes bodies tick. When I was that age I had no idea. My education on these matters was non-existent. When you are brought up with 'that' subject never being mentioned – without frowns and between pursed lips – you get the message. You are forever left with the feeling that sex is taboo to even think about, let alone discuss. The only time my mother ever mentioned sex was just before I got married: "It's just something us women have to put up with, dear." I feel so sorry for her now if that's what she had to do.

Naturally, there is a physical side to every couple's life. We started from scratch when we were first married, with very little previous experience to draw on. Sex wasn't a thing I'd been brought up to be open about, so it would be almost impossible to explain what I needed, and why it was important to me.

In all honesty, did I have any real idea of what I might enjoy or what physical pleasure could be all about? It's difficult to write this without feeling sad that such a wonderful act loses the magic that it should have between two people. I think it does require both parties to be able to talk about 'it' openly, but neither of us did. How could we? We didn't actually know what to talk about.

I have to wonder if more verbal communication might have improved matters. When you are inexperienced, you actually don't have a bloody clue what to say, let alone do. You might read books on the subject and learn from them, but if you can't discuss it then you end up as we did. We must have done something right though as we have our two lovely girls.

We never did get a honeymoon and life from then on was about keeping our heads above water, and having just enough money to pay the bills, with me working full time whilst my new husband finished his degree. After he graduated, we moved to Scotland to start his first job. The catering company that was employing me at the time was able to transfer me to their Scottish division.

In those days the journey from Cardiff to Glasgow seemed a very long one. When we eventually moved, I remember our car, a Mini-Traveller, being stuffed full with all our worldly goods. We travelled up to Glasgow a few weeks beforehand to have a scout around and look for somewhere to live. The rain was coming down hard when we started on our return journey. That was bad enough, but then the windscreen wipers decided to pack up as well. The torrential rain persisted all the way from Glasgow to Cardiff.

They say necessity is the mother of invention, so, finding a ball of string, we cut lengths of it and attached them to each wiper blade, threading the loose ends through the passenger and driver windows – leaving a small gap – which allowed the strings to be pulled from the inside. Being the dutiful wife and co-driver, I was delegated the task to be in charge of manipulating the wipers so that my husband could see where he was going. Every time I nodded off he would give me a sharp shove in the ribs because his visibility was cut short. When he nudged me the wipers would go frantically for a few moments until I remembered what I was supposed to be doing.

Every fifty miles or so we had to re-string the blades, as the string had frayed and snapped with the force of being tugged against the metal frame of the car. On reaching Cardiff several hours later, my arms were in spasm and my clothes were soaking wet where the water had been continually trickling down the strings. My biceps had improved a lot, though!

Several years later, when the children were still very young, we were still only just managing financially.

At one stage I was working part time in my husband's business, leaving home after the children went to school and returning when school finished. My job title was 'Office Manager' but being a small business, I did everything from data preparation, answering the telephone, sales, cleaning, to general dog's body.

I also worked Friday nights, Saturday, and Sundays at a local sports centre, cooking bar snacks and providing cricket teas, etc. When the children were a little older, they often came with me. Often my husband came home on a Friday night just as I was off to work.

On top of this, I worked two nights at the Family Planning Centre in Glasgow. Life was such a struggle yet still I put so much pressure on myself to complete the tasks that each day brought. My health began to suffer.

As the children grew a little older, we still needed my income. I started working as a catering manageress at a local garden centre and enjoyed it for a year but my dream had always been to have my own tea shop and bakery. I came across an advertisement in the local paper, 'Tea Shop and Bakery for Sale', and decided to find out more.

The bakery was situated in a small village about twenty minutes from where we lived. My husband encouraged me to go for it. One of the big disappointments about taking on the bakery was we'd have to move. We had to put our lovely house on the market and live in a flat above the shop. The children could still commute easily to their school by bus. The offer went in, the house went on the market, and we bought the business. It was a traditional bakery and looked like a chocolate-box picture. The shop was characterised by a stone floor and beamed ceiling. The tea room was on the first floor, reached by a steep twisting staircase. This area would seat no more than a dozen people.

Its name, *Muffins Bakery,* suited it perfectly. When all the cabinets and shelves were fully stocked, it looked so charming. The amazing mixture of smells wafting from that little shop ranged from fresh bread and homemade cakes to the aroma of freshly ground coffee. There was a delicatessen counter where we sold homemade sausage rolls, pizza, quiche, and a selection of cheeses and cold meats. Jars of jams, chutneys, and exotic pickles with brightly painted labels announcing their contents were arranged haphazardly on shelves. There were old tables covered with red and white chequered cloths; on them we placed hand-crafted biscuits and cakes arranged in wicker baskets. This for me was like the picture of roses growing up the door of a country cottage. In reality, it wasn't as idyllic as it seemed.

The business didn't have the best start. We soon discovered both dry and wet rot in the bakery and flat. This led to a further outlay of several thousands of pounds before we had even started. Eventually, both the bakery and tea shop were very successful. However, I found myself working a seven-day week, up at five and finishing at around nine at night. I was knee-deep in pastry, sponge mix, and meringues from dawn to dusk. What on earth was I trying to prove? I was killing myself.

There was no kitchen in the upstairs flat – the bakery kitchen had to serve for both the bakery and my family's needs. In addition to this, on one wall in our small downstairs sitting room I had a two-tier baker's oven, probably four to five feet across.

In the kitchen, there was a huge 'Hobart' mixer and racks stacked high with meringue shells and pastry cases for the coming week, plus bowls and utensils everywhere. Initially, the family thought it was wonderful coming home to the enticing smells and being able to help themselves. Unfortunately, there was no getting away from it; I was sweating sausage rolls and homemade soup. The small chicken or beef joint I roasted for Sunday dinner was cooked in the huge baker's oven and most nights the family dined on either pizza or quiche that I'd made for the deli counter earlier that day.

My husband had suggested employing a baker to help me, but any we interviewed wanted to use pre-prepared mixes for all the cakes. On my part, I felt I would have failed by using mixes and I knew in my heart the reason the bakery was doing so well was because most of the cakes were homemade. Eventually, my husband's sister joined me in the kitchen and between us we just about coped. This situation became even harder when it got busier and after just a year, recognising that my family and I were suffering, we decided to sell up.

Life had become competitive and materialistic; money became so important, as did perfection. All these obsessions were destructive and eventually I recognised how out of control my life was. Once on this particular treadmill it was so difficult to get off, but off I got. I had to; my body wasn't going to take much more.

After 'Muffins' closure and recognising that the children were now teenagers, and there was little for them to do in the village, we decided to return to where we'd been living before. At least they would be back with their friends and closer to Glasgow. The weird thing was the lovely old semi that I'd hated moving from was on the market again. We put in an offer and managed to buy the house back at less than we sold it for. What a relief it was to be back in that house. The estate agent showed us around, pointing out features such as the cupboard under the stairs with me replying, "I know, we lived here a year ago." The decoration, carpets, and everything else were exactly the same. I hung all the pictures up on the walls in the same place they'd always been. It felt like finding a pair of comfy slippers that I'd lost for a year and was putting back on.

Over all the years that I had worked at being a mother, wife, and breadwinner along with trying to fulfil other people's expectations, I believe I often undersold myself, my capability, and my potential. Sometimes this was lack of confidence, sometimes fear, and sometimes necessity.

Above all, I'm a grafter. Only after my marriage did I dare to channel this energy and tenacity into my own growth.

Chapter 12 – Health

It was twenty-three years into our marriage that the cumulative effect of three jobs, a family, and the pressures that I had put on myself to achieve 'perfection' started to take its toll.

I experienced bad palpitations, shortness of breath, and headaches. My body was telling me to ease up, but I wasn't listening to it. Eventually, I was referred to a cardiologist, who decided in all his wisdom to put me on beta-blockers for a year.

This did calm me down, but felt strange because my heart usually bobbed along around one hundred beats per minute. That's very high I'm sure, but was caused by what I was doing in my life. The consultant informed me that if my heart continued at that pace, it would wear itself out within five years so he convinced me that beta-blockers would slow it. They did and after taking the lowest dose I could my heart went down to fifty-eight beats per minute within a few days. This made me feel desperately ill for months from the side effects of these tablets.

I suffered for years with chronic health problems. I felt I'd even been allocated my very own seat at the doctors' surgery. In my own mind I was viewed with neither sympathy nor understanding there. The inevitable hospital referral came. They didn't know what was wrong so passed me on and on. The hospital was a series of endless corridors with directional coloured lines. The smell of cooked cabbage and disinfectant clung in the air. The consulting rooms were windowless boxes with a body-part picture on the wall; a wooden rack full of leaflets; a skeletal model on the desk; two bins containing yellow bags; and a sharps box endorsed with a skull and crossbones. It didn't inspire me.

Doctors came and went, examining, prodding, scratching their heads and staring at screens – "I think we ought to..." –

"we will just test for..." – "I think we should refer you to..."

I was sent from one department to another: X-rays; scans; blood tests; biopsies; exploratory operations; urologists; gynaecologists; neurologists; and any other -ologist that was available! By this time the only bloody -ologist I needed was a psychologist! Pricked, poked, prodded, and then passed on. Irradiated and invaded. Enough was enough.

The whole experience made me feel terrible, even though all my symptoms were very real with photo and X-ray evidence backing them up. I began to think people were whispering behind my back saying, "This woman must be suffering from hypochondria." After numerous doctors not looking at me as a person, just a set of symptoms, and not linking my symptoms to each other, I decided to look for an alternative way of treating myself. This route was to be homeopathy.

For two years I attended a homeopath in Glasgow. Though the homeopath did manage to relieve some of my symptoms for a short while, all of them returned again a few months later. She seemed to be treating my physical symptoms, but not helping me on an emotional level which is what homeopathy does so well. I needed both.

I'm not sure why we never got down to an emotional level. It must have been very difficult for the homeopath because whenever I saw her 'The Face' was always on – a combination of make-up and a smile all the time, laughing and acting the fool. That was me; no wonder I never seemed to get the right remedy and she tried so many. I must have been a confusing patient. In truth, I wasn't being honest with her and she didn't stand a chance of helping me properly. More fool me.

My poor experiences with conventional medicine have been repeated throughout my life. There have been times where without it the repercussions would have been disastrous. That said, alternative medicine can give so much more – the time to talk – a sympathetic ear without interruption. I've had two very good therapists and for me they played an important and supportive role during a very bad time.

Chapter 13 – 'The Face'

I wasn't a capable, strong, or independent person during my marriage. Thinking back now, my initial impression of myself is of somebody with little self-confidence, low self-esteem, fearfulness, vulnerability, and just about every other negative characteristic. Yet, on the outside people saw me as this cheerful, caring, happy-go-lucky kind of person with a big smile on her face. How wrong they were. I would get up in the morning and before anybody saw me I'd already showered, dressed, and put on 'The Face'. I know now 'The Face' was just the mask that I was hiding behind, rather like a clown. There I would be busying myself, breakfast made, house tidy, everything in its place but never having any time for myself and maybe not wanting it, just in case I had to stop and actually think. That would only make me feel worse. I always said to myself when this, that, and the other was finished, then that would be my time. It never happened. There was always something else to do or something I would find to do. Time for myself was never a priority.

My house was homely. It was warm and cosy, always a hot meal on the table, or a cake in the oven. It was like my castle. There I stood looking out into the unknown world, encased and isolated, unable to grow. As time went by the walls around my castle became higher and I became less and less willing to venture beyond them. I think that home wasn't so much a castle but more a prison of my own making: losing more confidence, feeling unbelievably vulnerable, wanting and needing the security and safety my four walls offered me. For years I'd felt invisible, almost part of the furniture, always being there for everyone else. I was the safe reliable caring person, despite always needing reassurance from family and friends and often not getting it. When anybody said "jump", that's exactly what I did. I feared that if I didn't they might not love me any more. Living in my family's shadows, I got joy from their achievements and lives. However, it was almost as if I was unable to match myself to them. They were intelligent, bright, and able achievers. As for me, well, I was just me – a wife, mother, and hard worker. I felt almost unworthy of being one of them.

When my children left, all that seemed to remain was a house, not a home, even though I tried so hard to keep it a home. Jodie, my dog, and I spent many an hour together waiting for life to get better. We walked for hours each day until she got too old, then we sat together, just being there for each other. I cared for her and she gave me unconditional love in return. Our bond was such that she seemed to understand my feelings and those large brown eyes bored deep into my soul. Our house was large with several comfortable rooms but most of my time was spent at the kitchen table. Maybe that's because the dog lived in the kitchen. Perhaps it was because the chair was hard and uncomfortable and I felt that was all I was worth?

When I did something just for me, not for anybody else, it was usually a Sudoku or a crossword in the daily paper – thus proving to myself I was at least a little intelligent. Even then I sometimes left the last couple of clues. I would ask my husband to finish these crosswords already knowing the answers but wanting him to feel good. There I was again putting myself down and needing to feel I was bottom of the pile. *How is it possible to understand all this now?* At the time it was just another of those little games I played. This one was called 'How to make your husband feel good about himself by demeaning myself'.

The other thing that was strange was that even when I spent time on my own I still felt guilty about having time for me. I never read a book during the day; I would only allow myself half an hour in bed before going off to sleep. There were times when I really wanted to finish a novel, or had come to an interesting part, but the book was put down and not picked up again until the appropriate time. If my day wasn't busy I felt guilty. I hardly ever sat down except for my meals and the odd cup of tea. The other thing I hated was being quiet so there was always background noise, either the radio or television. I'm sure the reason for this was when it was silent I had to think, and it felt extremely uncomfortable when I did.

Chapter 14 – The perfect wife

It was a cold winter's morning, around 6.30am. After placing a pan of milk to warm on the stove for my husband's breakfast, I pulled on my wellies and armed with a big bowl of warm water started to defrost his car. My eyes fell on the container of ashes at the side of the house where I'd cleared out the fire from the day before.

Measuring roughly how far apart the wheels were I proceeded to make two tracks up the hill with the ashes, to help the car to grip. I ran out of ashes halfway up and decided to go to the back of my neighbour's house and pinch some of hers. She was a good friend and I felt sure she wouldn't mind. Having made tea and packed up some sandwiches and homemade cake, I went through a checklist of what my husband may have forgotten. He departed with a peck on the cheek into his warm, defrosted car.

What a perfect wife I was. All through my marriage I defrosted cars, made endless packed lunches, warmed several thousand gallons of milk, packed hundreds of shirts in tissue paper so they wouldn't crease. I cleaned shoes, ran baths, and warmed water for his countless shaves, knowing it would save time as hot water didn't come out of a tap instantly in those days. The heating system we had was a little archaic; the immersion heater took an age to warm up and there were no timers either. Once, I even fished through a whole bath looking for his missing contact lens, unsuccessfully putting jug after jug of water through a sieve.

I must say that this was my problem not his; the pressure I put on myself was enormous, *but why?* At the time it was what I did. It never occurred to me to question my behaviour and ask myself what I was doing or why I was doing it. Always making sure there was cake in the tin, toad in the hole on Mondays, smoked haddock Tuesdays, shepherd's pie Wednesdays, followed by baked rice pudding, stew and dumplings Thursdays, and fish and chips on Fridays. I spent endless weekends helping with cricket teas, making countless cakes and sandwiches, and then of course washing up afterwards. If I had to go out, I always made sure my husband was well catered for, leaving a plate of sandwiches covered in cling film on the side in the kitchen with a note guiding him to the right tin if he required biscuits or cake.

Knowing his routine before he left for work, I would place two Shredded Wheat in a bowl, milk in a jug ready in the microwave. As soon as I heard the bedroom door close, I went into action, and by the time he arrived at the kitchen, the milk was the right temperature to pour over his cereal, a mug of tea already placed next to his bowl. Sandwiches, juice, fruit, and cake already prepared and wrapped, shoes cleaned, and if it was a cold morning, scarf, coat, and gloves were warming on the radiator. Looking back, I resembled the whole cast of 'Upstairs Downstairs'. I did occasionally play mistress of the house when work colleagues or 'important' people came for a meal, or to stay.

Most of the time when my husband was at home he would be in his study or watching sport and I would be in the kitchen with the dog or on a small settee watching a separate television or reading the newspaper.

Was I a wife or did I just make myself a slave?

Chapter 15 – The Isle of Man

After living in Glasgow and the surrounding area for more than 25 years we uprooted and moved to the Isle of Man.

I found myself on an island in the middle of the Irish Sea away from daughters and friends to start a whole new life. Me, the dog, and a part-time husband who was spending most of the week working on the mainland, and just 'visiting' at weekends.

Once I settled, the Island felt like the safest place on earth. In the summer it was so beautiful. Carpets of wild flowers and hedges of wild fuchsia. Each part of the Island so different, ranging from mountains, moorland, rolling hills, and magical glens, sea lapping the shores; some sandy, pebbly, or just sheer rock. The water appeared to change colour with every tide and cloud formation, and, as the sun dipped below the horizon, it almost looked as if it was lighting a stairway to heaven.

According to legend the Island was formed when the Irish giant Finn McCool lobbed a huge piece of earth from what is now Northern Ireland at another giant in Scotland. Finn's aim was poor, and he missed. The rock landed in the sea becoming the Isle of Man. I prefer to believe that the Island is made up of a little of Scotland, Ireland, England, and Wales. It has the ruggedness of Scotland, greenness of Ireland, the patchwork quilted fields of England, and a coastline like some of Wales.

The winters though were very different. They brought high winds, rough seas, rain, and mist. I began to dread them. I felt isolated from the rest of the world and when the mist was down it was claustrophobic. It could be rather frustrating at times. One year I ordered a turkey for Christmas. Most of the shop's supplies came from the mainland on the ferry. Mine was ordered to arrive for Christmas Eve, but that year the boat was cancelled because of rough seas. From then on I always bought a frozen one or found a supplier on the Island.

My health wasn't improving. I needed to find a new homeopath. I found Sam after checking out the British Society of Homeopaths in London, and so I made an appointment with him. I arrived early, as usual. Five minutes before my appointment, I got out of the car and hesitantly approached the premises. The garden was surrounded by a picket fence and the gate was metal with a brass sign and several letters after his name. The sign caused me to rethink the wisdom of the unconventional approach I was taking, but reassured by the normality of the friendly dogs stretched out in the garden, I went in. I pressed the bell, and, knowing the homeopath was male, wondered what he would look like. The picture in my head was that of a stout man, long grey hair tied back, wearing a kaftan, beads, and sandals who would greet me with the peace sign. The door opened, and to my surprise he looked completely normal. Tall and casually dressed. He greeted me and ushered me into a room.

The room was light, warm, and welcoming. I could hear the faint noise of someone clunking around in another room. It was reassuring to know someone else was in the house.

There was no tick of a clock. *Where was the clock?* I expected the homeopath could check it, without being too obvious, when the appointment needed to come to an end. That was how I felt about myself; I was wasting someone else's time, even though I was paying for the appointment.

On the table next to me sat a box of paper tissues. *Was I expected to cry during this consultation?* No chance! The first visit seemed to take an eternity. By the end, it was me looking at my watch, wanting it to finish. At the next convenient pause in the conversation, I opened my cheque book and asked to whom I should make it payable? A bit rude of me I thought, and Sam looked a little shocked.

After several visits, I began to trust him and feel that I could open up a little. Sam served as a valuable guide through a three-year journey that was to change my life. Before long I found I was asking myself more and more why I acted the way I did. I was thinking things out and coming to conclusions that I didn't like, but eventually they had to be addressed. All these thoughts and feelings I was suppressing, *how on earth had I not been able to identify the way I ticked?* However, as time went on I started to understand myself.

The consequence of my perfect housewife routine was sadly to be a divorce. I did realise that striving for perfection came from my relationship with my father, but it wasn't the solution to my marriage problems. He'd set the benchmark of my worth and now it was coming back to bite me. When my husband and I started to discuss and address things, I found myself answering more and more honestly. Life almost became a battle. I was resenting my life and how I'd behaved. My husband seemed to know exactly what he wanted. Whenever he said, "I want to go and play golf", or do some kind of course, somehow my answer to him would always be, "That's fine, you do what you want as long as it makes you happy." Underneath, I was seething because I wanted him to spend time with me but was unable to tell him. If I had asked, no doubt he would have done something I wanted to do. The unhappier we became the more we seemed to retreat into our own worlds. Our expectations of happiness ran too high. It seemed the only common link we had was our family. I knew we were in trouble and I'd realised years previously that I wasn't happy, but didn't know what to do about it, so carried on as I was.

The realisation that I was unhappy had resulted in an incident when we were still in Glasgow. The children were barely teenagers, and I'd been out somewhere. On returning home, the family were waiting for me to organise dinner. They'd done nothing to help, all just getting on with their own thing as usual. I'd allowed them to get used to the routine of me doing everything, so it wouldn't have occurred to them to prepare a meal. What a martyr to their cause I'd made myself. In a fit of absolute fury, I rebelled, acting like some spoilt child stamping its feet, telling them there were baked beans in the larder and asking them sarcastically if they could handle a can-opener. I then packed a case and advised them that I was going to stay with my sister for a while. I was petrified about what I was doing. There were no mobile phones in those days. It was a cold, dark winter's night. I got in my old car and drove from Glasgow to Wiltshire. I'd reached my breaking point.

I'll never forget my family's faces watching out of the kitchen window as I reversed out of the drive. My daughters were looking at me in utter bewilderment and shock. There were several frantic telephone calls from them over the next few days. I returned a week later. Did I learn from that experience and go back a different woman? No. I took the easy option to stay in the marriage and have the security that it brought.

As time went on it became increasingly difficult. I used to dread my husband coming home to the Island as it felt so awkward. Our relationship was so unstable. I found his time with me almost an intrusion. He made more and more excuses to stay away: I encouraged this.

This couldn't go on.

Chapter 16 – Beginning of the end

In December 2005 the wedding of our youngest daughter loomed large. 'Loomed' is probably not the best word to use. She was so excited, and there were many arrangements to make. It should have been one of the highlights of my life, as it was when my first daughter got married; I had been a proud and delighted Mum. Their marriage ceremony was to be held in a beautiful rural church on the Welsh borders. The wedding would be made even more special by the fact that a familial uncle was officiating at the ceremony, with the reception afterwards at a wonderful old manor house hotel a few miles away. We were living on the Island then, as were the bridal couple, so organising things at a distance was a little difficult. A short while before the wedding we'd purchased a house in Yorkshire as a base for my husband, and a place for me to stay when coming to the mainland, so I'd been there for a few days. I'd driven all items needed over from the Island that week. On the Friday before the wedding, I travelled over to the hotel to settle in for the happy event.

Of all the things that had happened during my marriage, this was the most testing, unhappy, and devastating: my husband and I had decided that after the wedding we would be separating. Keeping this secret from my daughter and her partner was very difficult. I knew if I shed just one tear of joy the flood gates would open, so I had to stay composed. There was no way the impending separation between her father and I would be allowed to upset her. I confided in my sister, who bore the brunt of it. My homeopath Sam and his partner also knew of my troubles. They helped a great deal with suitable remedies and sympathy. My elder daughter was told only the basics of the collapse of our marriage as she had a ten-week-old baby, our first grandchild, and enough to contend with. I discussed with her the advisability of telling the bride and groom but we decided in the end that it was best to say nothing. This was a time when above all others, I had to maintain the 'FACE' in capital letters. The usual smile for everybody, but this day I was dying inside.

For the sake of appearances my husband and I shared a room, which added even more strain. How he was feeling I don't know as there was little discussion between us. The atmosphere was best described as frosty.

Guests started arriving during the Friday and into the evening: my future son-in-law's family, my other daughter, her husband, the new baby, and the bridesmaids. I smiled until my face and jaw ached with the effort.

The day of the wedding arrived, bright and sunny, just as I had to be. The morning flew by with hairdressing appointments and last-minute tweaks. I did all the mother-of-the-bride things and at least, at this point, a little tear was appropriate. My daughter looked beautiful. I left her with her father and went off with the bridesmaids.

I walked into the church filled with so much emotion and tension. I could hardly breathe; my ribs ached as I held myself tight. I was grateful to be able to sit down for a while, but the silence in there made me feel very emotional. The bride duly arrived and was escorted down the aisle by her father. She looked stunning and I was so proud of her. My little girl was starting her new life today. The ceremony proceeded without a hitch and the happy couple, arm in arm, returned down the aisle. This was by far the worst moment of my life. How ironic that her father and I had started off together walking down the aisle and, thirty-six years on, here I was walking down the aisle on the arm of my son-in-law's father, knowing that my marriage was at an end. I can't even remember the music or the smiling faces, just this overwhelming feeling of not being able to breathe and needing to get outside for some air. It felt as though I had just gone through the divorce in my own mind.

The photographs, confetti, congratulations all passed in a

blur, but I do remember a couple of comments to the happy couple. "We hope you do as well as your Mum and Dad, forty years together, that will be a real achievement" and" So nice in this day and age that your parents' marriage has been so happy. A good foundation for you." *How wrong could they be?* I wanted to scream, tell everyone that they were wrong, I wasn't happy. No one knew what was going to happen next. *How could I spoil my daughter's day and honeymoon?* My sister was there in the background, but apart from telling me how lovely the bride and I looked, she avoided all contact with me. She knew I would have collapsed in a heap at a reassuring word or cuddle. We all had to keep up this pretence.

At the reception I sat near my husband on the top table. The speeches came and went. I can't recall hearing what was said about how I had raised my daughter. With the formalities over we continued into the evening reception. My husband and I were sitting at different tables. This was probably for the best.

Perhaps the next day would be easier. We wandered into the breakfast room with the guests. Everything appeared normal; everyone was so happy, people drifted from table to table chatting, smiling and laughing. The smell of a full English breakfast tempted the most hung-over.

I felt sick, not sure whether my stomach was in my throat or my shoes. I did eat something, what, I can't remember but even in these circumstances, the planner that I am, I knew that it would be much later in the day before there would be another opportunity. To face this day wasn't something to do when feeling light-headed with hunger. My smile was firmly in place and outwardly I hoped I showed no signs of my inner turmoil.

The day passed in a flash: bride and groom, hand in hand, waving off the departing guests, packing up their car and ours with presents, dresses, suits, cakes, cards, and luggage for the honeymoon. My husband and I, together with our daughter and her new husband, would be driving to the airport, where they would fly off. We'd drive the two cars back to the Yorkshire house. It had been arranged that we'd pick them up from the airport just before Christmas and take them back to Yorkshire for a cosy seasonal celebration. Well, that's what they thought.

We set off in convoy to the airport, my husband and I driving in silence. On getting out of the car to see them on to their flight, the 'face' went on again, and I made a tearful goodbye to the newlyweds, who seemed totally oblivious of any tension. Off they went. I got into our vehicle and my husband drove theirs. The wind blew, and the rain came down heavily. It was like the end of the world was coming. I drove along the motorway blinded both by the rain and my stinging tears. I wanted it all to be a bad dream but sadly it wasn't. At one point I remember thinking please, take this all away, hoping that some idiot of a driver would cross the carriageway and hit me head on, thus ending the pain I was feeling. I'd never have the courage to end my own life, but at the time, and feeling the way I did, I wished that someone else would.

The plan was to stay in Yorkshire overnight and then I'd return to the Island in our vehicle with all the belongings. My husband would stay put and I'd return to Yorkshire closer to Christmas. By the time I arrived at the house, I was in pieces, eyes red from crying and shaking. I tried to talk to my husband, seeking some kind of resolution, but we couldn't find the words. However, he did come back to the Island the next day to help unpack what had been needed for the wedding and then immediately returned to Yorkshire, leaving me with all the reminders of the wedding.

How on earth was I going to deal with Christmas now? As a family, we'd decided earlier in the year to have a quiet Christmas day in Yorkshire, then on Boxing Day all the family would travel to my other daughter's house in Newcastle to celebrate the rest of the season with them and their delightful new baby. How perfect it would be. How perfect it should have been. Now though, it was too late for the newlyweds to change their plans. I insisted that my husband should collect the couple from the airport after their honeymoon and break the news of our separation, explaining to them the reason why. This he duly did. What an awful homecoming for them. They'd have been expecting to arrive to a seasonally decorated house, the smell of mince pies and ham cooking in the oven, with me there to greet them and hear all about their time away.

It was impossible for me to make that happen, even for them. There was no way that I could put my 'face' on again and pretend that everything was wonderful, that her father and I were truly still friends. To spend a few days, even a day, in the same house as him would have been too difficult for me. Rather than cause huge upset to plans made long before, I talked to my elder daughter saying that I really didn't want to cause her any problems, so her sister, new brother-in-law, and father would still come up, but that I'd find somewhere else to go over the holiday. She tried to tell me it would all be fine but no, I didn't want my girls watching every action and reaction between their parents, even if it was only for a short time. I thought it would take the pressure off everybody if I wasn't there. I knew that I needed their love and support at that time. Quite honestly I felt it should have been their father who went elsewhere, but as usual I put their feelings first instead of my own.

This putting myself down meant that I was suppressing my own needs – never finding out who I was and what I was capable of – and so missing out on much of my own life. Now my comfort blanket was about to be pulled from under me, and I was on my way to a divorce. *Was it me that instigated this?* At the time it felt that my husband left me, but now I'm not so sure. *Was it inevitable?* He needed excitement, wanting to know what it was like not to be married, and the reassurance that old age didn't mean a pipe and slippers. For some reason I wasn't what he wanted any more.

Though I desperately wanted to be with my family, I did what was right for them and went to stay with my sister for Christmas.

Chapter 17 – Break up

Whilst writing and reliving those days, I can see that I'd become a 'giver' and was living with a person who was happy to receive. I wonder if I'd ever been strong enough to stand on my own feet. I realised I was always hiding my own natural desires and needs. That probably made matters worse in the end. If I'd felt able to express these feelings to my husband, then possibly we wouldn't have reached this point, but I wasn't. My upbringing was, in many ways, the cause of my downfall. My father's attitudes dominated me and I craved praise. As it was with my father, I just kept on trying to please. I had become the housekeeper and it wasn't enough for either of us. *How could it have worked?* Especially when you feel you are taken for granted. Our relationship seemed one-sided. *Who is at fault? Is it me for being what life had made me?*

I was devastated. I just wanted my life to be safe and secure again. What was to follow was a terrible time. My husband moved across to the mainland permanently. I was left on the Isle of Man with a house to sell, separation agreements, solicitors, and accountants to deal with. This was done in a haze of confusion, anger, and disbelief, wondering what I would do next. This separation felt almost like a death.

We decided not to contact each other. I was stuck in this terrible abyss, paralysed by fear and vulnerability. I wanted someone to take all the pain away and tell me what to do. I know grief is a natural part of separation and that I'd have to honour it, feel it – but there was the temptation to try to anaesthetise myself. I realised there was no short cut. The only way out was through it. Believe me, it was scary to feel the fear and try to move on.

My husband came back to the Island several weeks later on my elder daughter's birthday. He was armed with a transit van to pack all his belongings and take them back to the UK. *Was this really happening or was I having a nightmare?* My younger daughter and her husband, so recently married, offered to come to the house and support me, knowing how difficult this would be. I thought this would probably be the last time I saw my husband. It was very difficult for my daughter being placed in this position – after all it was her father and she was stuck in the middle.

What terrible times these were. Not just for me, but for both my daughters, their husbands, and close family. Everyone was stunned. Particularly affected was my husband's elderly father who used to stay with us in the winter months for ten or twelve weeks of the year. He telephoned me and asked why we had separated. He was crying, asking who would now make him oxtail stew and dumplings. Although I understood his meaning, at the time it felt as though food was more important than my feelings.

Not only was my marriage ending, it was also breaking relationships with people I'd known for forty years. The extension of my family was my husband's family with whom I had grown from a child into a woman. *Would those relationships fade because it was too difficult? Would it cause problems for his family to continue to be close to me? Did people feel they had to take sides?* The ripples of the break up went on and on. *Was I to start a brand new life with no connection to my past?*

After loading up all his belongings, our home was gradually being dismantled. The study half empty, large gaps in wardrobes, CDs removed from racks, things being loaded into the van and leaving huge holes everywhere. Our home was becoming merely a house again, losing its identity. I was in utter shock, yet I still made cottage pie for dinner. *What was I thinking?* We sat at the table in the kitchen; he opened his laptop and showed me a photo that he'd entered into a competition. *How could he do that?* He was leaving me. This was probably the last time we'd ever be together, and he was looking at photos. He spent the night at my daughter's house and returned the next morning for our visit to the solicitors and accountants. I was told the first visit to the solicitor was to arrange for a separation agreement to be put in place.

Winter on the Isle of Man could often be overcast, wet, and windy. That morning was completely in context. The sky was heavy, with dark rain clouds and the wind whipping the waves into a frenzy in the bay. White horses were dashing towards the shore, then crashing into the dark stones of the sea wall. There was a sense that the world was coming to an end, and I felt as if it was. We found a parking space easily in the multi-storey car park and walked the short distance to the solicitor's office, my husband striding on ahead with me desperately trying to keep up. I'd hoped there would be time before the meeting to discuss what would happen but that wasn't to be. I had no idea what he was going to say.

Chapter 18 – Facts and figures

I've thought a lot about how to describe that meeting with the solicitor and just how much it affected me. I felt unprepared for it. We had not discussed any arrangements regarding finance, future sale of the house, where I would live – all the things that need time, thought, communication, and some sort of agreement between the two of us. I naively went into the solicitor's office without any idea of what was to follow.

We were ushered into a small claustrophobic room with no windows, which seemed no bigger than a broom cupboard. It had only two chairs and a desk with a solicitor sitting behind it. The image of a police interview room came to mind. The solicitor looked younger than my daughters, probably fresh out of university. *How could this young woman have any idea how it felt to have known someone for forty years and then not have them in your life any more? What experience of life would she have at her young age?* In fairness to her, she was there just to hear the separation agreement arrangements and note them for preparation. She wasn't there to advise either of us; that would be a matter for our individual solicitors once it was drawn up. At the time though, it was just another thing that helped to set this awful scene and to undermine my confidence even further.

I know that divorce is a time for making arrangements for the future and that there are many aspects of a long life together that need to be agreed upon. Hence the separation agreement in which both parties eventually decide on what is to happen and how. In that small claustrophobic room, I felt overwhelmed by the details that needed to be sorted out. The process stripped any emotion out of forty years of being together. It ignored all that I'd done to help, support, and love this man.

Not having had the slightest idea of what I was to be

confronted with, and hearing all the details for the first time, I suppose I went into shock. I couldn't speak and certainly couldn't think straight. The solicitor seemed to think that I agreed with all that was said, which wasn't the case at all. I needed time to recover and somebody to help me sort this out. I said that I would need to get my own solicitor to look at things. I was already feeling sick, weak, and wobbly, hardly able to stand. There were so many emotions going around in my head.

The meeting finally finished and, still reeling from the effects, I went with my husband to the accountant's. We weren't only husband and wife, but business partners in several businesses. This also needed unravelling. I had no knowledge of what was to be done to dissolve the partnerships or any financial repercussions that might ensue for me.

Eventually, we went back to the house for him to carry on packing his belongings. I felt angry, sad, confused, vulnerable, unloved, and rejected. I now looked at him with pity. It was the only emotion that I had left. He sat in his usual armchair. I realised I no longer looked up to him as I had for all those years together. I'd begun to see him differently. What a difficult few hours those were until he finally went.

Chapter 19 – The start of moving on

Life was very tough during the next few months. The pain and rejection that I was feeling went on and on. Days passed, each one seeming more like a week. I was on a roller coaster of thoughts, feelings, memories, and plans, beside myself with grief, aching for the huge part of my life which had been lost. I constantly felt terrified about what lay ahead. I found myself doing irrational things – wanting to steam open credit card statements to try to decode what he was up to. I feel certain that many people going through a separation would feel tempted to do the same and recognise how I was feeling. Certain music, smells, and sounds brought back painful memories. Talking to our mutual friends was now on a different level. Almost all were insignificant conversations like, "How's the weather?" They became minefields because I knew it wasn't possible to mention my husband. If I did, it was to cunningly get clues about how he was and what he was up to. I compared myself to a real life 'Hercule Poirot' and I'm sure had I continued down this route it would have driven me crazy. At least I didn't resort to cutting the legs off his suits or vandalising his car, but it did cross my mind. I do remember, at one of my lowest points, wishing I had done something like that. The world around me carried on but I felt as though everyone was treating me as if I had some sort of contagious disease. I often wondered if he realised just how much he had changed my life.

As the weeks went by I considered that anyone going through bereavement would feel like this, except it was a living bereavement. I'd lost my warm blanket and my companion. I felt raw, alienated. Sometimes just getting from one hour to the next was tortuous. Eventually, though, I found there were small moments in the day when I was actually not thinking about him. I'd take a sip of tea and find myself laughing involuntarily at something on the television.

These little pockets of hope began to knit together and I started to focus on good things as a respite from the bad.

That was how I saw him then. In reality he had never been my warm blanket or my companion, as I wish he could have been. I think that was my image of what I wanted our life to be, like the cottage with roses growing over the front door, the perfect family. The marriage was never like that, no matter how much I tried. I could provide the warm cosy house, and always something nice to eat, but that wasn't enough.

Don't get me wrong, I wasn't perfect, often something would snap in me, especially just prior to the separation.

One of those times I was in the kitchen, busy ironing my husband's shirts, something I'd always liked doing. Ironing board up, tea made, biscuit on the side, and usually finding a television programme that I liked to watch. My husband wandered over, intently watching what I was doing. He stood there for several minutes. I was thinking he wanted to tell me something. Then he said, "Will you show me how to do that? I suppose I should learn, as I might have to do it myself." I was horrified. I'd carried out this task for the last thirty-six years and he hadn't once offered to help. All of a sudden he was thinking ahead, knowing he may have his independence, so now he was going to learn.

I felt as if I was falling at speed into this dark place where I didn't want to be, but I showed him. *What the hell did I do that for?* He proceeded to iron his shirt. I think he then expected me to take over again once he had finished. I was so angry that I told him there were another six shirts in the basket, and as he had now mastered the skill I'd never iron a shirt for him again. I shouted and screamed. I remember taking a plate out of the cupboard and throwing it to the floor near him for full impact. Even though I felt out of control, what did I do? I found the oldest, odd plate in the cupboard to throw – not my best china. He turned around looking a bit bemused and said, "I can't believe you're reacting like this, over just ironing a shirt." This showed me again how far apart we had grown emotionally.

My emotions seemed to be all over the place. I really lost it, although I was still in control. I made a quick exit out of the front door, slamming it hard for effect on the way. I got into the car, the tyres screeching as I took off at high speed. I drove like a maniac. I found myself parked up in a secluded spot next to the sea. It was dark. I sat with the window down watching the moon dance on the water and listening to the silence broken only by the sound of waves hitting the sea wall. I wondered if I was having a nervous breakdown.

I could have stayed in that place forever, but it was getting cold and I knew that I had to face up to what was happening. Eventually I returned home. My husband greeted me with, "Have you calmed down?" There was no answer to that.

My marriage felt like a game of chess. There we were, both waiting for the other to make the 'wrong' and the 'right' move. There were no right moves that day and it felt like the bill had finally become due, no getting out of paying now. I tried to work out what had gone wrong. *Did we reach a plateau?* So many thoughts went through my head, but I had no idea what to do with them.

It took a long time for me to figure out that we were on different paths. With the distraction of work and children, I was more focused at home while he was always excited about the next opportunity ahead. I realised that with the children older, I'd begun to change as well. Maybe that was part of the reason he left. I was no longer the safe, caring person he married – I was looking for more. We ended up being two people living in the same house, with two separate lives, and, as time went on, growing more and more apart.

In retrospect, I'm not bitter or vindictive, just very sad at the lack of togetherness we ought to have shared for all those years. I thought we had both been satisfied and content with our relationship for such a long time and that we were doing all we could to meet each other's needs. The sadness is that for some reason there was never the open communication between us that makes a marriage work. Neither of us had enough confidence in the ability of the other to understand how we saw things, so it was never discussed. There must be a thousand reasons why these sorts of barriers come between two people and some manage to overcome them, but we didn't.

It's perhaps inevitable that, in the end, one or other of you decides that you have grown so far apart that there is no point in continuing the relationship.

I felt totally cast aside, chucked out with the rubbish, and left to make what I could of my life from then on. Yes, I was all of the things that you would expect at that time: bitter, hurt, lost, bewildered, but not destroyed. There was more to me than that. If he could move on, then so could I.

When you are that far down, the only way is up and wallowing in self-pity is no way to start climbing. If I'd thought about what the next part of my journey to my new life would entail, then I'd probably have never started. My reaction would have been to shut all the doors, barricade myself in, and let the walls around me grow even higher. At this time I'd have said that there wasn't a chance that I could achieve what I then managed to do. Rather than fail, I wouldn't have begun, but this time, I did.

Chapter 20 – TV to India

Not long after we separated I was ironing, with the television on in the background for company. I wasn't really taking much in, just in my own little world and wondering what was going to happen to me: how I'd cope now I was on my own. The programme on was *This Morning* and in the distance I heard Fern Britton, who was one of the presenters, talking about something called 'The Challenge of Your Life'. She was inviting female viewers to write in with their stories and the reasons why they would like to take part. Applicants were requested to submit a brief synopsis of their lives and explain how they'd benefit from this challenge. Fern explained that *This Morning* was to choose two women to cycle across Northern India, 'Rajasthan', adding that she would also be participating. A further six women would be chosen to take part in two other challenges, but the nature of these wasn't disclosed at that time.

I was really feeling sorry for myself, so thought, *What have I got to lose?* The frame of mind I was in at that stage, it didn't occur to me to worry about any possible danger I might put myself in. I just didn't care. Life at that time was terrible. I couldn't sink any lower. I scribbled my story on three sheets of paper, crossings out, the lot, and posted it.

I went to Glasgow for ten days to prepare and serve a buffet for a hundred and forty people at a British Superbikes function. This was a commitment I'd agreed to months earlier, and, not wanting to let anybody down, I decided to fulfil this obligation even though my heart wasn't in it. On returning home, I opened my front door, tired after such a hectic few days, and picked up my post from the mat, not intending to do anything with it for the moment. However, I noticed an envelope with the logo of *This Morning* on it and opened it immediately. I expected it to be a 'Dear John' letter saying thanks for applying, but no thanks.

103

I'd been short-listed from tens of thousands of entries. It was such a shock. This kind of thing didn't happen to me. At the time it was just what I needed; coming back to an empty house and receiving such good news was a real boost. The letter invited me to a selection day which was to take place on Saturday 5th August 2006 at the ITV Studios in London. The day itself was to consist of informal chats with the producers and the *This Morning* team of experts consisting of psychologists, life coaches, counsellors, and a keep-fit expert. It didn't take many seconds to decide that I was going to do this. Wow, somebody wanted to know me better. It was a 'bring it on' moment.

I travelled over on the ferry a couple of days before, then drove down to the West Country to stay with my brother and his wife. I needed to be at the studios by 10.00am, so I boarded a very early train on the Saturday which was a direct line to Paddington and then a tube ride to Waterloo. This was a challenge in itself, not knowing London and where the ITV studios were located. After receiving directions from a rather unfriendly soul at Waterloo, I decided to walk to the studios along the Embankment as it was such a lovely day. I arrived about 9.45am. What a massive building. As I entered reception, my knees began to knock. I was feeling very nervous but then reassured myself, what do you have to lose? Absolutely nothing. Just enjoy today – so that's what I did.

There were a few women sitting on sofas. We all had our photographs taken, were issued with clip-on passes, and were signed in after producing our passports. Everyone seemed so excited. I found out there were sixty-three women short-listed. It was quite a humbling experience talking to these women. Their stories were amazing, and I wondered why the programme planners had chosen me to be one of those sixty-three. One particular woman aged twenty-six had been diagnosed with cervical cancer and was now in recovery. Another twenty-eight-year-old had just gone through breast cancer. One woman was in an abusive marriage; another woman's son had recently died. *What was I doing here?* A divorce seemed nothing compared to what some of these women were struggling with, life-threatening diseases. Though thinking about it, I suppose after the length of time I was married, divorce was as much of a life-changing experience, albeit in a slightly different way. We were all facing our own very personal and private 'challenges'. I told myself this was why I'd been picked.

Mid-morning we were divided into groups. The rest of the day consisted of talks with a life coach, exercise classes, and informal chats with a counsellor and psychologist. All these experts were to decide whether they felt we could confront the physical exhaustion and mental challenges that would lie ahead of us. A film crew followed our progress all day. After a buffet lunch, we all gathered together and were told that they'd chosen thirty women from the original sixty-three. They called out the names and, to my utter amazement, I was still in there!

The afternoon was a repeat of the morning, further talks and exercise. The day just flew by. It was fun, but very tiring. At the end of the afternoon we were informed that the producer would contact us in a few days to let us know if we had been short-listed further.

I was due to return to the Island in two days. I decided to pick up my messages remotely from my home telephone, and to my amazement a message had been left by the producer of *This Morning* saying I was one of those being called back. We were now down to fourteen women. I was invited to go back to London the day I was due to return to the Island, for a day of fitness. Oh boy! I had a sleepless night, thoughts running through my head of what that might entail. I telephoned the producer in the morning for details about where we were to meet. They'd chosen a hotel in Central London which had a gym and swimming pool. She asked if I could bring clothes to work out in and a swimming costume. What was that all about? Having not returned to the Island, I had no swimwear with me. When she asked me to go and buy one, confirming that the show would reimburse me, I thought they must be keen!

It was very short notice but I managed to book a ticket to Waterloo. The train left at 6.10am prompt. The producer had instructed me to arrange a taxi from the station, again saying they would reimburse me for all my expenses. I was beginning to feel very special – expenses even! All fourteen women had to be at the hotel for 10.00am. The train that morning only managed to get me as far as Swindon; a message across the tannoy advised there had been a points failure at Basingstoke, so there was going to be a long delay. Typical, all this exciting stuff happening in my life and here I was sitting on a train with the situation totally out of my control. I contacted one of the ITV team to inform them. They said, "Don't panic – just get to the hotel as soon as possible." Those comments made me feel so much better.

There was another message over the tannoy. This one advised that we were travelling to London via Southampton. Surely that's going in the wrong direction? Panic set in again. I'd be fortunate if I managed to get to London by lunchtime at this rate. I was sitting opposite a lady, table between us. She looked as if she was probably in her fifties. Beautifully dressed, laptop in front of her, mobile phone by her side. I thought she was obviously a career lady – high powered, very confident, and upper class. I assumed she was totally unapproachable – thinking she was a rather 'plum in the mouth' sort.

I had two options. I could change to another train and wait at Swindon – we were told this could be a long wait – or stay put and travel to Southampton. Having no idea what the best option was, I thought this lady looked like a seasoned traveller, so very gingerly decided to ask her advice. She suggested Southampton would be the best choice as this had happened to her in the past. To my surprise she was nothing like I thought. She was very nice. In fact we seemed to gel straight away and even showed each other pictures of our first grandchildren. She enquired why I was going to London and seemed very supportive about what I was doing. I found out a little about her too; we exchanged telephone numbers, and she asked me to keep in touch and let her know how I got on. All my life I've made assumptions about people by the way they look or speak, the 'cover and book' syndrome. How wrong I was about her? Lesson learnt for me. Read the book, Jill, read the book.

I finally got to the hotel at 10.45am, only three-quarters of an hour late. After checking in with the receptionist, I was directed to the swimming pool. By the time I arrived all the other women had changed and were in the water. The whole place looked like a film set. Bright lights surrounded the pool, sound engineers and film crew hovered. I was beginning to wonder whether this was a good idea. No make-up and a body that looked a similar colour to a pint of milk. *What was I doing?* I was shown where the changing rooms were. I came out with a towel covering me from neck to knee hoping I could sneak in the water without anyone noticing. No chance! The cameras followed me from the changing rooms to the pool. Once the towel was off I tried to place my hands and arms discretely across my middle, feeling very self-conscious, bending like a half-open penknife hoping they'd miss my middle bit.

It got worse. We were then asked to swim thirty lengths of the pool doing front crawl with our heads under the water. Why were we being asked to do so many lengths anyway? I wondered what the other challenges were. I cannot do crawl, and, even if I could, I'd never put my head under. My head stays up when I swim breaststroke, never ever getting my face wet. I must be the only woman who can go swimming and get out of the pool with dry hair and her make-up still on.

After coughing and spluttering whilst explaining that I really couldn't do front crawl, they told me not to worry – do thirty lengths using breaststroke, which I managed. That was just the beginning. After a quick lunch at the hotel, we were then introduced to the gym and spent the rest of the afternoon either on a running machine, bike, rowing machine, or stepper. Maybe this was how they'd choose – the women left standing would take part in the challenges!

We were advised at the end of this that the team wouldn't make a decision that day but at 5.00pm we were all asked to gather in reception. The whole film crew were there – apparently they'd made a decision. They wanted two ladies to ride 420km across Rajasthan (Northern India) and eight to do two other challenges. We later found out four ladies would be running in the London Marathon and four would be swimming the English Channel. Thank goodness I couldn't do the front crawl!

Julie Dawn Cole was going to be personal trainer for the two ladies going to India. She is probably best remembered for her remarkable performance playing Veruca Salt opposite Gene Wilder in the 1970s movie *Willy Wonka and The Chocolate Factory*. Later in her career she qualified as a fitness instructor and worked on various projects, including 'The Challenge of Your Life'. Julie stood in front of the team and said, "Jill, you are going to India." She handed me some cycling shorts and a pot of Vaseline. I was completely stunned, total disbelief on my part. I turned around thinking there must be another Jill amongst the women, but it was me. I was crying, shaking in shock from head to foot. *Was this really happening or was I dreaming? Why did they choose me?*

It seemed that nothing had ever happened in my life where I felt it was *me* who'd actually succeeded, and now I had been chosen to take part in this challenge, not because of my husband or family, but just ME in my own right. It had often been commented on my school reports 'Jill tries hard', never 'Jill has done well'. Having my potential recognised was very empowering. Susie, the other woman chosen to ride with me, seemed equally surprised that she had been selected. After several glasses of champagne and a few canapés, Julie said, "Make the most of it girls, after today your training starts seriously."

I was chauffeured in a limousine from the hotel to Waterloo station. The chauffeur was given strict instructions to make sure I got on the right train. Just as well because after several glasses of champagne and very little lunch my head was spinning, legs like jelly. I was on such a high. What an amazing thing to happen. My life would never be the same again.

Arriving back in Wiltshire, my sister and her husband were there to welcome me. I was so eager to tell them everything. They drove me back to my brother's house, where I was staying. It was late and during a restless night's sleep, each time I woke up I had to pinch myself to realise that the day before had really happened.

Chapter 21 – Training

The next day I went back to the Isle of Man. A cancelled train and ferry crossing delayed by three hours due to engine failure meant that I arrived on the Island in the wee hours of the morning. My feet didn't touch the ground from that moment on. I discovered further details about the Challenge. Not only was I cycling 420km across India, but Fern, Julie, Susie, and I were joining ninety other women on this trip to raise money for Professor Lord Robert Winston's charity Women for Women Appeal, which funds research to improve the health of women and babies. As participants, we'd each have to raise a minimum of £2,800. I had three months to get fit and to raise this money somehow. *Could I really do this?* It was a challenge in itself.

The same week, Julie started organising my fitness schedule. This was to include not just cycling but getting totally fit. I had a long way to go. The limited experience I had of riding a bike was as a child, and because of the amount of cycling we were doing in India, there was no time to waste. I found a personal trainer, joined a health club with a swimming pool, and of course got 'THE BIKE'. That was my first priority. Thankfully, the people on the Isle of Man were very generous, giving free time and membership for the few months of my training. The fitness schedule put together for me consisted of:

Swimming at least twenty lengths three times a week.

Working out with a personal trainer for about forty-five minutes two or three times a week.

Cycling: building up from three to fifty miles every day, aiming for one hundred miles over two consecutive days.

The following week, the producer of *This Morning* accompanied Julie over to the Island to film me training. What training? I'd only just got a bike and my fitness schedule organised. This was moving too fast, but on reflection with only ten weeks to go, I had no choice but to accept what was planned. The team duly arrived at the airport and using a local film crew we all headed for the promenade in Douglas. It was raining quite heavily. Julie, who was upbeat in the worst of conditions, proceeded to cycle down the promenade with me, giving useful tips on my training programme as we pedalled. Feeling soggy, but full of new inspiration, we cycled back to my house, all the time being filmed by the crew and hoping that the shots they got, particularly when they were behind us, were acceptable. In the afternoon I gave my very first interview for the programme. That was so scary. In my head all I could hear was "Lights, camera, action". Thank goodness it only required one take.

From then on I started training in earnest, out in all weathers every single day. My challenge was picked up and championed by the local press and I became a bit of a celebrity on the Island.

My day started with a bicycle ride just after sunrise. Cars hooted, people shouted encouragement, and bikers waved. That was the nice thing about living on the Island – people were always so friendly. My days consisted of exercise, exercise, exercise. The cycling was usually on my own, although sometimes at weekends I was joined by my daughter and her husband. After advertising locally for a cycling companion, I teamed up with a lady who was also taking part in the Women for Women India challenge. We often arranged a day's cycling together. As it was mostly just me and the bike, I decided to give it a name and called it 'Soli', short for Solitude. 'Soli' became my best friend.

Often, I swear I could hear him calling me at 6.30am from the garage. The wind would be howling and rain pelting on the bedroom window. All I wanted to do was pull the duvet over my head and go back to sleep, but I resisted the temptation. Dressed in waterproofs, helmet, and gloves, I looked like someone in a biological hazard suit. After a few tentative stretches, I was off – armed with a few nuts, a banana, and some water. Unless you've ever experienced the way the wind can blow on the Island, you can't imagine how it felt early in the morning, trying to battle against a strong head wind coming off the sea. I'd talk to 'Soli' all the way and not once did he answer me back, thank goodness. Soaking wet, with rain running off my waterproof trousers into my trainers, it was a case of stopping to eat a soggy banana and a few nuts, a gulp of water, and back on the wet saddle for even more miles. *Was I crazy?* – Who knows?

I was very much into homeopathy at this point due to my poor experiences with conventional medicine, so the next stage of my preparation for this challenge proved to be very difficult for me. I was told I needed a course of vaccinations before I was allowed to travel to the remote areas of India planned for the cycle ride. I really didn't want them but was informed in no uncertain terms that if I wanted to continue to take part in the Challenge, I had no choice. Apparently I couldn't be insured unless these were done. I received the first set of vaccinations, consisting of hepatitis A, typhoid, polio, tetanus, and diphtheria, using both arms. By 10.00pm the first night, my arms felt like lead weights, I was so tired and ached all over. By virtue of its remoteness that part of India is inhabited by a large number of rabid dogs and monkeys. Experts had decided that I'd also need two shots of rabies vaccine as well as malaria tablets and, to top it all, the meningitis vaccine. *Would my body ever forgive me for contaminating it with all these toxins and would it ever recover?* The days after my first shots left me feeling terrible.

By the end of the first week's training, vaccinations included, I was up to eight miles a day. By the end of the second week 'Soli' and I managed eight times along the promenade. I knew from the milometer on the bike that this equated to fifteen miles. With the regularity of cycling this

113

route, I knew every pothole in the tarmac, every missing railing from the fence, and how many dustbins and dog bins there were. I even counted the street lights. I began people watching – making up lifestyles for the occasional pedestrians. Were they married, maybe having an affair? The latter would be difficult. To keep a secret on the Island was almost impossible; you couldn't even sell a house without the local paper declaring how much you sold it for.

Now my saddle was beginning to feel very uncomfortable. My bum hurt! 'Soli' and I cycled down to the local bike shop, where I'd purchased him from, to ask for expert advice. Maybe I wasn't carrying enough fat in that area or perhaps the saddle was rubbish. Surely my rump would start hardening up soon and things would improve? We were taking the saddle we trained on to India. The owner of the shop said that for the number of miles I needed to spend sitting on the saddle, it wasn't appropriate and ordered me another one.

Covered in bruises and feeling numb in regions I'd prefer not to talk about, I decided to forego cycling for the day. Instead I went to see my personal trainer at 7.30am and later swam twenty lengths of the pool. I finished by walking four miles. It was only lunchtime but already I was ravenous. I know exercise increases your appetite, but this was ridiculous. Let's hope, I thought, by tomorrow I'd no longer have a numb bum.

A few days later the owner of the bike shop telephoned informing me that the new saddle had arrived. 'Soli' and I cycled to the shop in Douglas where the owner fitted the saddle. He measured everything and assured me that the old one wasn't high enough. I thanked him and off I went. My toes could only just reach the ground and I felt decidedly unsafe. It was fine when there was a kerb, but with no kerb and nothing to set my foot on to, off I came, straight into a flower bed. I pulled leaves and twigs from my jacket and helmet. Then I swore at 'Soli' and cycled on as if nothing had happened, hoping my unladylike dismount hadn't been viewed by too many people.

Scattered amongst all this training were visits to the ITV studios where Susie and I were interviewed to update viewers on our progress. Travel arrangements were made for me to fly to London City Airport on the Sunday. The remaining successful applicants who'd be taking part in the other challenges would be appearing on the following day's programme. This would be my first time on live television. A driver met me at the airport and took me to a hotel in Central London. ITV would be paying all my expenses. Wow! How good was this? I was informed that I'd be picked up early the next morning and taken to the studios where my make-up would be done. Not sure I fancied going anywhere without that. At least the limo had tinted windows.

On Monday morning I awoke early with a pounding headache and upset tummy. All I could put this down to was chronic nerves. I was picked up at 8.00am, looking as though I hadn't slept for a week. Breakfast would be available in the 'Green Room'. Breakfast? The thought of food made my stomach turn somersaults again, but nonetheless I still felt important because I'd heard loads of celebrities talking about the 'Green Room'. This is where the guests gather prior to going on set. I wondered who I'd meet, me with no make-up on and feeling like a wrung-out dish cloth.

On arrival at the studios I met up with Susie and the eight girls taking part in the other challenges. We were to be filmed outside and luckily it wasn't raining. The programme was to include the launch of 'The Challenge of Your Life', as well as revealing to the eight other women what their challenges entailed. After filling in a few forms with regard to the legalities of appearing on television, we changed into our T-shirts emblazoned with 'The Challenge of Your Life' logo. Then, after going to make-up, we were escorted outside on to the Embankment to film the opening shots for the programme. This consisted of running with some rather fit-looking male models to the music of the 'A Team'; every girl's fantasy. So this is what it's like on the other side of the screen. Nice!

Next, we were ushered back to the 'Green Room'. The odd thing was, it wasn't green at all. It was soft sofas, tea on tap, cakes, croissants, sandwiches, and fresh fruit, and the television monitor, which would show us the progress of the programme. I was sitting with the other girls awaiting our television debut at 12 noon. Another round of make-up, toast, and tea before watching the opening of the programme which included the selection process for the Challenge, plus the section we had filmed out on the Embankment that morning. How strange it felt, watching myself on television.

The guests in 'The Green Room' that day included Paul Burrell and Chico. They were so nice. Thirty minutes prior to going on set I was starting to quake. I asked if I had time to dash to the ladies but was told I didn't. The nervous bladder would have to wait. A young man complete with headset, clipboard, and trainers, known as a runner, ushered us through to the live studio and before I knew it I was sitting in front of the cameras with Fern Britton, Philip Schofield, and Julie Dawn Cole asking me how the training was going. I must admit, they were all super. Their relaxed manner made us forget we were being watched by millions of people. The other girls were told what their challenges were: four to run the London Marathon and the other four to swim the English Channel. I was pleased I was unable to do the crawl. I like swimming but prefer the safe jellyfish-free confines of a pool. After lunch in a small bistro just off the Embankment and a further chat with Julie regarding my ongoing training, a driver picked me up and delivered me back to the airport. I could really adapt to this kind of lifestyle. How special I felt.

It was nice to have a rest from my saddle for a few days but it was now mid-September and we were off to India on 15th

November. Only eight weeks left to train. The next day, I was tired but 'Soli' and I were on the road again. We were up at 6.30am and out by 7.00am. I needed to be back by 8.15am as I'd been asked to do a live radio interview with BBC Wiltshire. They'd telephoned me a few days previously, as they'd picked up my story and knew I was moving back to Wiltshire soon. I was also doing an interview with a local Island newspaper. If there had been forty-eight hours in the day, it still wouldn't have been long enough.

All this was going on but I was still trying to sell the house, deal with a divorce and everything that went with it, see a personal trainer, a physiotherapist, have further vaccinations, and I needed to raise nearly £3,000 in the form of sponsorship.

In addition I was dealing with all the emotions and thoughts running through my head. I had a supportive circle of people around me. Thank heavens for my family and friends. What would I have done without them?

By mid-September 'Soli' and I were up to twenty-three miles most days. I was still swimming twenty lengths of the pool three times a week, with a little bit of aqua-aerobics here and there. There was also regular physiotherapy because of pre-existing back and neck problems, exacerbated by the relentless training. All in all, I was doing OK and with every passing week I was becoming much fitter. I had energy levels that made me want to go on forever. I hoped it would last.

One evening I was cycling along the promenade. It was busy. People were sitting on benches eating their takeaways. I was speeding along the cycle track and someone threw chips for the seagulls. One swooped to pick them up and I hit it with my front wheel. I turned back to view the results of the accident. There were no loose feathers or sign of the gull. It had obviously flown off but on returning by the same route later, I spotted a seagull with a limp. Was that the one I'd hit? It could still fly, so I felt a bit better.

I wrote letters to local firms on the Island asking for help to raise money for the sponsorship. The lady I had met on the train on my way to the studios that day – the one I had thought was a 'plum in the mouth' sort – sent me a cheque for one hundred pounds. That was so very generous. The companies my daughter and son-in-law worked for sponsored me. At the time I worked for the Family Planning clinic on the Island and a few of the staff there donated. The Isle of Man Steam Packet Company also kindly gave me a hundred pounds. It was a very good start to raising the sponsorship required.

It was becoming incredibly difficult to juggle everything and when I write this now, I don't know how I managed to survive. *Where did I find the strength and determination?* I can't believe what I was doing. The house was up for sale. I was trying to keep it tidy for viewing. I was also keeping up the training and starting to pack up the house before moving. I'd put a deposit down on a new-build house about three miles away from where my sister and brother lived in Wiltshire. My brother and his wife had offered to put me up in their home for as long as it took for my new house to be completed. I knew the area very well. I felt I'd be safe and comfortable there.

As the weeks went by, and the impending India challenge loomed closer, there were lists everywhere of things I had to do by when. I had garage sales to sell miscellaneous items that I'd decided not to take to my new home. I was trying to raise a bit of desperately needed cash. Boxes and mess everywhere, trying to do some packing in between cycling endless miles. By the end of September, I was up to thirty miles every other day. Come rain or shine I was out there. I was beginning to resemble one of those before and after photographs from a body building magazine. I'd developed calf muscles like balloon sculptures and walked as if I'd been riding a horse for several weeks.

After my first thirty-mile ride I arrived home, grabbed a piece of bread, opened the fridge door, and helped myself to a large chunk of cheese. I ran the bath and got in. I woke up an hour later immersed in freezing cold water holding on to a soggy piece of bread with cheese floating in the bath water. At times like that I longed for someone to be there, to take me under their wing and care for me – an arm to hold and support me. Someone to say, "It'll all be ok."

I was keeping a daily video diary, which I sent to *This Morning* on a regular basis. They would choose which bits to show their viewers on how I was progressing. I think it was for the benefit of any sadist who got a kick out of seeing another human being suffer. I'd mastered how to operate the equipment but the first attempt captured me with half a head and a sink full of dirty dishes in the background. Eventually, it just became another item I had to tick off on my daily schedule – just another part of my preparations.

Chapter 22 – Challenges

This Morning set up other challenges for me to take part in before going to India. The first one was at the end of September 2006. I was flown from the Island to Gatwick. The flight was delayed because of bad weather. Yet another challenge: taking off into a gale-force wind. It was difficult, to say the least. Arriving in one piece at Gatwick, I boarded a shuttle bus to the Thistle Hotel. As I checked in, there was an American gentleman standing behind me in the queue at reception and to my utter surprise he asked if I'd like to join him for dinner. Not having been introduced or even exchanged names, I politely declined his offer, though felt a little flattered. He was quite presentable. However, being slightly concerned about bumping into him at dinner I ordered room service. Maybe it should have been chicken?

The next morning my driver collected me. Not knowing what my challenge was or where I was going, I tried to find out. Nothing would induce him to reveal our destination. I was feeling a little anxious, remembering that when applying for the Challenge, I'd said that I'd do 'anything'. My worst fear would be to either jump from a plane or perhaps go wing walking. Stop it Jill, they wouldn't dare, would they? We could be going to a zoo and I could be asked to let a giant hairy spider walk across my hand. I shivered at the thought.

We arrived an hour later at a large country park. There was a notice which advertised 'Paint Balling'. Maybe that was it? We drove a little way into the estate and came to a halt in front of two large wooden gates which were blanked off and offered no view inside. A man came out of them and instructed the driver to wait until all was ready within. He informed me that when they opened there would be two people waiting to greet me.

Ten minutes later we went in. I discovered that Julie was one of the two. The other was a chap dressed in combat gear.

Julie and I were asked to run along a narrow footpath through trees and dense undergrowth, followed in hot pursuit by some mad army instructor shouting at us to get a move on. In a clearing we were given combat gear to change into. It consisted of overalls, hard hats, and fingerless gloves. Next, we were marched to a clearing on the other side of the wood. It was an army assault course. Please let me out! ANYTHING BUT THIS! I might be much fitter than I was a month or two ago, but this was ridiculous – me a woman of fifty-six. How on earth could I possibly complete a course like that? To make matters even worse, the clothing that I'd been given was made for a six-foot gorilla and not a dainty little thing like me. I was in constant danger of losing my dignity and kept having to hitch my breeches up!

The course was laid out starting with a raised ramp to launch ourselves off, grabbing a rope to swing across a deep ditch filled with cold, muddy water. I silently prayed that my upper body muscles that I'd worked so hard on would hold me up and I wouldn't end up in that water. Then we crawled under criss-cross wires, through metal tunnels buried in the mud, under nets, stepping in and out of large tyres, climbing over logs, hanging on to a large rope bridge, and last, but not least, a ten-foot high wall with ropes attached to the top, no foot holes. *Was I supposed to get over that?* I'm 5'1½" tall. I looked on in utter horror. Please tell me this is a nightmare and I'll wake up in a minute. All this and dressed in a romper suit many sizes too big.

This was being filmed, with Julie doing the course too, and she was very fit. Afterwards, Julie commented how even she'd found it a struggle... but I did it!

Horror of horrors, Justine, the producer, said there had been a problem with the filming first time around and we would have to do it again! If I'd had the strength, I'd have hit her. By the time I'd completed the course for the second time I was so tired. Bruises were already beginning to appear, but that wasn't the end of it. We'd only just got to lunchtime and there was still the afternoon ahead of us. We couldn't wait!

Julie and I sat eating our lunch, aching but strangely happy at our achievement. She looked at me and said, "You're still wearing your wedding ring." It was such a simple statement but something that had been troubling me for a while. I had taken it off a few times but somehow the band went back on after an hour or so. I felt safe when I was wearing it, still within the confines of a marriage. That sounds daft, I know, but I suppose the most prominent feeling was that of a kind of comfort blanket. It was my protection against becoming single again. I wasn't sure I was ready for this new way of life, though I'd have to adjust eventually. I said to Julie I was getting there and she nodded knowingly. I felt she understood and I didn't need to elaborate.

After lunch Julie and I were put in a Land Rover and driven across a bumpy field. Julie asked me to cover my eyes. What next? After being guided out of the Land Rover, my eyes still tightly closed, we walked up a bumpy track. Complete silence apart from the noise of bushes rustling and birds singing. I was told to uncover my eyes. If the camera and sound crew hadn't been there then a few choice words would have come out of my mouth. In front of me stood a thirty-ton tank! The instructor from the morning session and another army guy were there, dressed in combat gear. They asked me if I'd ever driven a tank before. As if! I replied, "You're not going to ask me to drive that thing, are you?" Of course, the answer came back, "Yes."

My first challenge was to get into the tank. It was at least two and a half times my height, if not three, and not a ladder in sight. After being given a rather unladylike push up from the dashing instructor, I tumbled head first into the driving compartment. There were two separate compartments, one for the driver and another situated behind. I suppose in combat that would be for a soldier to use the guns. There was a huge gun on the tank but I was told it wasn't armed. Shame, I could think of a few people I could have used it on! The instructor showed me how to drive the monstrosity, a huge clutch pedal, brakes, and gears but no steering wheel – just a metal arm you moved left or right. He sat in the compartment behind and we were linked by radios connected to our helmets. Because it was so noisy we had earphones on as well. I think I looked a bit like Goldie Hawn in *Private Benjamin*. Some chance!

I was in total control of the tank. I turned the engine on and with the instructor shouting from the back, off I went around a huge cornfield. This was very empowering. It was great fun being encapsulated in something so strong. I felt safe. After several circuits of the field I thought I'd mastered it and felt as if I could conquer the world. It was physically quite demanding to drive, and after the assault course in the morning I was beginning to feel absolutely exhausted. We came to our last round and I was bombing along. The instructor, who also owned the tank, told me how to halt. The camera crew decided they wanted some good footage, so they got a cameraman to lie in the field in front of where they wanted me to stop the tank, not leaving me much leeway. As I tried to depress the brake pedal I found I just didn't have the strength to do so. Sheer panic was setting in, so I tried to pull on the handbrake, but still the tank wouldn't stop. All I could see was the cameraman lying in the field. Thankfully, the instructor made a swift exit from his compartment, pulled himself across the top of the tank and lowered the upper part of his body into my compartment. He physically pulled the handbrake on even harder. It's a good job he reacted so quickly, otherwise I shudder to think what could have happened...

We sat on top of the tank and Julie then interviewed me for the programme due to be broadcast the following week. I told her I wished I could take the tank home with me but I didn't think it would fit in the garage.

"Never mind," replied Julie, "just drive me to the station!" We both put our helmets on to pretend we were going to drive away. I put mine on back to front and collapsed in a heap of laughter, so we had to do a retake. What an exciting day, and one I'll never forget. When this was all cut and edited for the programme they married up my driving the tank with the song 'Don't Stop Me Now'. Such a great choice to go with those clips. It's now 'Jill's song'. If I ever hear it, it fires me up and transports me back to that fun day.

I climbed out of my oversized romper suit. Having given the helmet and gloves back to the instructor, I just about managed to thank him for a most interesting day, then collapsed into the back of the car for the journey to Gatwick. The driver dropped me at the airport and once on the plane I fell asleep for the whole flight to the Island.

When I returned home I showered and went to bed. By then I was beginning to feel very sore. The next morning the alarm woke me at 6.30am. As usual, I tried to get out of bed, but couldn't move. I was covered in bruises and felt like I'd gone ten rounds with Mohammed Ali. 'Soli' could call all he liked this morning, I wasn't going anywhere. I got an appointment with the physiotherapist in the afternoon. He asked me if I had been in a car accident. When I told him what I'd done, he seemed more than a little shocked and amazed that I wasn't badly injured. After a few gentle pulls and twists I started to feel slightly better, but only slightly.

Chapter 23 – Leaving home

Time seemed to be steaming along and it was now the beginning of October, just six weeks away from the India trip. I was still off the target of fifty miles a day on the bike. Life started to become frantic, I also hadn't raised all of the sponsorship for the ride. It looked as though the house had been sold and, just to top it all off, I had more vaccinations to come. I felt I wanted to curl up and die as more and more pressure was piled on.

Because the Isle of Man is a country in its own right, having its own Parliament, laws, and currency, it wasn't just a matter of getting on a ferry and setting up home in England. I had to almost export myself from the Island and import myself to the UK. There were so many things to arrange – mail redirection, changing banks, taxing the car before I left the Island, changing insurance, and of course still dealing with the divorce.

The riding was getting harder and if I wanted to get to my target I had to be spending hours on my bike each day. Amanda, my cycling partner, lived quite a distance away, so with a bike rack fitted to the back of my car, I could drive to meet her. With her help, I managed my first continuous thirty-mile ride. It's so much easier when you have company. By mid-October I was up to thirty-eight miles, but most of my day was taken up sitting on a saddle, with little time for anything else.

One day there was a visit to the solicitor and lots of telephone calls to make. I thought at one point I should get a mobile phone complete with headset, so I could do all my business whilst riding 'Soli'. The same day the removal company were coming out to give me a quote for taking my goods across to Wiltshire. Plus, of course, I had the video diary to do, as well as training. Packing up my possessions, I thought: *When am I supposed to sleep?* Autumn was coming, and I needed to get some lights on the bike. It was now dark when I started training in the morning and when cycling later in the day it was often dusk on returning home. The only feedback I was getting was from my physiotherapist, commenting that I was in very good shape. He was impressed with the six-pack I'd developed and all those rippling muscles. Then, yippee, on the 15th October 2006, at exactly 5.21pm, my first fifty-three miles. I'd done it! Not sure I could do it again tomorrow though. Spending the whole day out on the bike, up hills, down dales I'd seen more of the Island than I'd ever seen before. By the time I arrived home, I could hardly move and didn't even have the strength to make supper. I found a bag of crisps, a banana, and a KitKat. I was in bed by 8.00pm.

My 'Guardian Angel', a dear friend from Glasgow, arrived on the 17th October and stayed until I moved. I was relocating to the UK on the 24th. What would I have done without her help and support? Not everything in the house was boxed up ready for storage. What a difference she made. As soon as she arrived, she got to work packing and organising. That was what I needed. She made sure I was fed, watered, and gave me a cuddle when I fell apart. We sorted out my clothes for the next six months, stuff for India, and things that could go into storage.

Before I left the Island, Julie and the film crew came across with Susie, the other rider. We were going to cycle the T.T. course. It's no mean feat. It's not flat but made up of several nasty mountains, all thirty-three miles of it. We left from the Grandstand where all the motorbikes start and finish the race. That part is nice and flat. We went on to Ballacraine, which really was like going up the side of a mountain, so steep it would have been quicker to have got off 'Soli' and pushed. At this stage I was only doing three miles an hour and it got worse. We were half dead, and when the allotted time for filming finished, we'd only managed two-thirds of the course.

A few days later I received a call from the producer of *This Morning* to say they would like Susie and me to go to London and be live on the programme on the 30th October. This was only sixteen days before going to India. We were told Pete Cohen, a well-known life coach, wanted to take us out of our comfort zones. Excuse me? What have I been doing over the last few months? I tried to guess what this might be. Did I tell them during all those interviews that I had a real fear of snakes and spiders? Please tell me I didn't. At this stage, there was nothing I wouldn't do – jump from an aeroplane, or even walk across hot coals, but please, please, don't ask me to hold a snake or hairy spider, otherwise I really will have problems.

My 'Guardian Angel' was still with me, and I could now see some spaces on the floor. The packing was coming together and there was order where there had been utter chaos. I was still cycling, going to the personal trainer, and swimming. In three days' time I was moving from the Isle of Man. Three more nights of total silence – no traffic – just the reassuring sound of gusty winds and feeling so safe here. Will I ever feel that again?

Monday, 23rd October 2006 was my last night in the house. Entries in my diary at the time show how I felt.

Just one more day on this Island: very mixed emotions, one door closing tightly shut and another opening. I feel so very sad today, knowing I can't go back, but grieve all the same for what has gone. It's not leaving my home that is making me sad but leaving the Island. My daughter and son-in-law are here, also some very good friends. Thank heavens my 'Guardian Angel' is here to look after me, someone to say good morning and someone to say good night to, I'm not sure how I'd have coped without her.

My last day in the house, I was up at 6.30am. It was just a shell – boxes and cases all sealed up. The removal company arrived early that morning. They were putting everything into containers and I was trying to load what I'd need for the next six months into my car to take across to England. My bike was, of course, going with me so I could continue training. 'Soli' would be secured on a bike rack on the back of my car. Once the removers had gone, we finished cramming the last few things into my poor vehicle, which was laden. There was only just room for me to get in. My friend and I cleaned the empty house for the last time. The home that I had put so much effort into was now cold and lifeless, with the heart and soul ripped out of it. It was now just a symbol of a failed marriage. I wished the new owners better luck than I had and drove off.

That night we stayed with my daughter and her husband, down in the South of the Island. The following morning necessitated rising at dawn, in order to catch the ferry across to Heysham. My 'Guardian Angel' was flying back to Glasgow, I was so sad to lose her. The worst part of all would be leaving my daughter and her husband on the Island; they'd been so supportive. My other daughter and her family, who lived in Newcastle, were also very supportive though it would have been difficult for them to be able to help as much, being so far away, especially as they'd only recently become parents to my lovely granddaughter. With the car packed to the gunnels, and just enough space to see out of the back window, I drove off in tears, trying not to look behind me. How alone I felt.

The ferry arrived at Heysham a little early. The weather was atrocious: wild, wet, and windy. That was probably the reason why the boat was forty-five minutes early as the wind was behind us. With optimism, I started to drive down the motorway, thinking I'd arrive at my brother's house by late afternoon. This was soon to turn into a bad dream. I was stuck in a traffic jam from hell, north of Birmingham. I managed to drive sixty-nine miles in four hours. It gave me time to question whether I'd made the right decision, but there was no choice. The house was sold and that was that. Would I always be fighting like this to get from A to B?

Tiredness washed over me, nobody to take the wheel, rain pelting down, wind moving the car as I overtook vehicles and 'Soli' still holding on for grim death on the back. It was as if someone was saying, "Let's give her more and more to see if she cracks under the pressure." I felt so emotional, cut off and vulnerable again. By now I was exhausted, barely coping with the atrocious visibility because of the heavy rain. I desperately needed to stop, deciding to pull in at a service station. As I did so, my mobile phone rang. It was the solicitor. Yet another problem that needed sorting out 'urgently'. At this stage after six hours of driving, four hours on a ferry, and getting up at 5.30am, I'd just had enough, so in the middle of the conversation I simply turned the phone off. I finally arrived after twelve hours of travelling. My family helped me unload. 'Soli' was put in his new home – my brother's garage.

I was so happy to have arrived. I felt very lucky that my brother and his family had invited me to stay with them. Leaving the Island and my family, it would have been awful to have had to go into rented accommodation alone, especially after that journey. The idea of nobody being there for me would have been too much to bear. As it was, my brother and his wife had a warm comfortable home and their family around them. They made me feel part of that with a cup of tea, a warm meal, and a shoulder to cry on. My sister and her husband lived next door, so I felt surrounded and supported. They listened, helped, and advised and were just there for me. It must have been very difficult for my brother and his family to have me staying in their house. As it transpired, it wasn't just for a couple of days but for several months. I was conscious of invading their space. How could they relax having me around all the time?

It was also difficult for me, trying to give them privacy. My space was the third floor of the house, which was very comfortable with television, double bed, and attic space to store my belongings. The bedroom also had the most amazing view over the town. Decades before, this used to be my parents' house. It was where I grew up, so naturally everything was familiar. As I awoke sometimes not quite conscious, I'd be almost transported back to my childhood when I'd lived there. It was difficult as this was where I'd met my soon-to-be ex-husband, so everywhere I went there were ghosts from the past.

It was 26th October 2006; I was now in Wiltshire with only twenty days to go before flying off to India. I'd become used to cycling on the Isle of Man and never having to think twice about my personal safety. I'd cycled through plantations and very remote parts of the Island, never looking over my shoulder. I was now in a very different situation and the way of life here wasn't the same. I had to work out new cycle routes to clock up the miles and make sure they weren't too remote. Maybe I was just feeling vulnerable and insecure? Even though I had grown up here it seemed so different from the Island: lots of traffic, so many people, just busy. So 'Soli' and I cycled mostly along the canal paths. The local gym proved to be very generous, providing me with free membership together with a personal trainer for my last few weeks before my trip to India. Nothing really changed very much with my training schedule, swimming at the local pool, plus aiming to cycle between thirty and fifty miles most days.

I continued trying to raise sponsorship funds and donations for Professor Winston's charity. The major event for raising this money was organised mostly by my sister, when I was still living on the Isle of Man. She'd spent weeks going around local shops and businesses asking for donations, alongside selling tickets for a fundraising dance to be held at the local rugby club with a prize draw, food, plus the appearance of four local bands. Thanks to my family most of this was donated. Julie Dawn Cole came down to run the auction and the event raised just over £1,000. With the help of so many people a grand total of £4,200 was raised for the charity by the time I departed for India.

Chapter 24 – Setting off

I was due back on *This Morning* a few days after the fundraising event. Arrangements for travel and hotel accommodation had been organised by the programme. I travelled up from Wiltshire the day before the show and stayed overnight in a lovely Central London hotel. I was wondering what the next challenge was to be. I was apprehensive after the assault course.

The chauffeur picked me up at 7.30am the next day. I had to be at the television studios by 8.00am, where Susie and I were to meet Pete Cohen, the life coach. We asked him what we'd be doing, but he said it was a secret. I knew that he'd be taking us way out of our comfort zones. Pete had already mentally prepared us for the worse.

As previously mentioned, I have a total aversion to snakes and spiders, which I'd succeeded in keeping quiet. I knew if they asked me to do anything involving them the answer would have to be no. I remember thinking, *I'd rather walk across hot coals.*

Susie and I joined Fern, Phil, and Pete Cohen on the sofa. There were no snakes or spiders, but I was told, "You are going to walk across a bed of red hot coals." I thought it was all a big con – pretend hot coals and a bit of acting. How could they risk us getting injured a few weeks prior to going to India? Astonishingly, it was no con. It was, possibly, poetic justice.

The runner escorted us to a large hanger downstairs. I asked Susie if she could smell burning. When we arrived, we were introduced to three men from a company called 'Men in Black'. This didn't bode well. Two were heating up coals in wheelbarrows and a third instructed us on how not to get burnt feet. A five-metre-long piece of turf was laid on the ground and they poured three barrow-loads of red hot embers on top. We were given further instruction on the technique and how to prepare ourselves mentally. The emphasis was 'mind over matter'. Yeah, right! Fern and Phil joined us for the second half of the live programme. The trainer threw paper on the coals to show the viewers how hot they were.

With Fern, Phil, and Pete on the sidelines shouting words of encouragement, there was no way of getting out of it. I wasn't over-enthusiastic. I looked at Pete and said that if he was so keen to get us to do it, how about he showed the way? As it was on live television, he had no option but to agree, so off came his shoes and socks. He did it and left me to follow. Off I went remembering to shout every time I put my foot down. I did it! Not a burn in sight, but my feet did feel hot. I'm sure there was a strange smell. Was it singed flesh or the evaporated perspiration of fear? It nearly made me change my mind about snakes and spiders. It was tough. Not quite as bad as snake cuddling, but very close.

That afternoon the *Daily Express* had offered Susie and I makeovers: hair, make-up, and outfits, then photographs taken. This was to be published in the 'Female' section of the paper the following week. I felt very special. It was a real pamper, which I needed after the last few tough months. I was hoping the makeover didn't include my feet, which were still black from walking across hot coals. For a few hours I felt wonderful. What a boost it gave me.

The feeling didn't last long. The next day I was back in full training mode again – pool first thing where I swam twenty-five lengths, lunch, to Bath and back on 'Soli' – twenty-five miles in two hours, a telephone interview for the *Daily Express*, dinner, video for *This Morning*, and then bed. *Please let this come to an end soon.*

At the beginning of November, I started to list the things I might need for India. There was so much on my mind – I wished I could just disappear. I didn't sleep well. A week after doing the photographs for the *Daily Express*, I got up early to go and buy a copy. There was a double-page spread of me and

Susie (nearly a whole page to myself), pictures and a write-up underneath. I didn't recognise myself dressed in colours I never wear, plastered in make-up, and perched on a stool. I felt that the clothes made me look overweight and the make-up aged me. I hid the paper under the bed and hoped that not too many people would see it. Obviously, there were comments. One of my daughters said, "You look nice." She meant that she didn't want to hurt my feelings by telling me the truth. My other daughter said, "It's a bit in your face, Mum." My sister added, "it's OK", which means it's not so good. I was conscious of everybody trying not to offend me.

By mid-November everything was getting so frantic. My life seemed to have been taken over by other people. One particularly bad day was Friday 10th November 2006. I got up early and cycled eleven miles along the canal. It was frosty and very cold. Everything ached. Next was a session with my personal trainer, who worked me very hard. The afternoon was manic: a telephone to each ear nearly all afternoon, if it wasn't the land line, then it was the mobile – the company who were building my new house, someone organising a photo shoot, BBC Wiltshire for a radio interview, *This Morning* to say they now wanted us in the studio before we departed for India, the solicitor to sort the separation agreement. My sister was running around, sending and receiving e-mails on my behalf. My head was pounding. I felt angry, sad, and tearful all at once. I cancelled the photo shoot and physiotherapist, because now I was off to London the next day. *Who else wants a piece of me?*

There was only a week left before the trip. The challenge had become not could I cycle across Northern India, but whether I could find enough hours to do all that was needed. I went to the camping shop first for a sleeping bag, plus a miner's torch to put around my head to enable me to see all those horrible bugs when I went to bed. Next, I visited the chemist for first-aid items, Vaseline to lubricate all those places that get sore when cycling, and suntan lotion. Then the general store for socks, cycling shorts, underwear, healthy snacks, nuts, energy bars, and chocolate. I wasn't sure my body could survive on curry morning, noon, and night. Packing for my time away was virtually impossible. After losing the plot completely on this task, kicking the holdall and trying without success to throw it around the bedroom, I made a bit of a racket. My sister-in-law took over and succeeded in packing competently.

I packed a further bag ready to go to London the next day for the final appearance on the show prior to departing to India. I really could have done without that. There was so much going on. I was trying so hard to keep myself together, but panic was setting in. Sam, my homeopath, sent me another remedy. Normally I take 'Tarantula'. How apt is that? In a couple of days I could be coming face to face with the real thing. I wondered how I'd feel when this was all over. *Will I feel lost, not having anything to focus on? Will I go back to being the person I was before? Will there still be fun in my life? What if? What will happen in the next few years? Do I want to know?*

I stayed in the usual hotel in London, but the chauffeur was late picking me up next morning, so everything became a little frantic. On reaching the television studios 'The Green Room' was very busy with Fern's other guests that day; Peter Andre, Katie Price, and their children, Michael Ball, some X-Factor contestants, and a sex therapist, who seemed to think that she knew me. I'm not even sure if I know what a sex therapist does!

It was a very emotional show. They'd sent a film crew to the Isle of Man and Newcastle to interview both of my daughters, who had sent good luck messages. Listening to them made me feel even worse; I was missing my family so much. Peter Andre presented me with a basketful of things I might need in India – more Vaseline and haemorrhoid cream. *What was that for?* There were also several other personal items, mostly to do with the rear end.

Two days later, my brother-in-law removed the saddle from my bike. I was taking it in my hand luggage to India, along with my helmet. I hoped having trained on the saddle that I'd be a little less saddle sore. I said a sad farewell to 'Soli', who was put away in the garage for a well-deserved break. How I envied him the thought of a nice long rest. I wasn't going to get one. I was about to embark on the biggest challenge of my life.

PART THREE

AFTER INDIA

Chapter 25 – Back to reality

I'd completed the India challenge and was still living with my brother and his family. The house on the Isle of Man had been sold. Unfortunately, we were still in the throes of a rather acrimonious divorce, and the money from the sale of the house was being held in a solicitor's account. I desperately needed the deposit for my new home to be available within a few weeks. Eventually, after several letters and heated conversations with solicitors and the like, I managed to get the money through. The new house was bought off plan, so apart from looking at site maps and choosing the best location from available plots, that was all the information I had. The houses were built on a slipway between the Marina and the Kennet & Avon Canal. My new home overlooked the Marina at the front of the property, and the canal at the back. The expected date for completion was May 2007 and it was now December 2006, so I still had a further five months to go.

I was getting impatient, longing for the independence of my own front door and new beginnings. I felt as if I was intruding on my family's lives, although they never once implied this. Without the focus of training and visits to ITV, I began to feel really low. I wondered where life was taking me, and if I'd be OK when I got there.

At my lowest, I wanted to be transported back in time to a place I felt safe and secure. *Was that place just the way I expected life to be? That place of my childish dreams.* As a little girl, I remember drawing pictures of houses with smoke puffing out of the chimney, pretty curtains at the windows, and children playing happily in the garden. There was always a washing line full of pegged clothes swaying in the wind. Even at that age that was how I perceived life to be as an adult and what I tried to portray.

The place I most wanted to be transported back to was the old semi-detached property in Glasgow. *What made that house the way it was – warm, cosy, and welcoming? Who lit the paraffin heater in the bathroom in mid-winter? Who cooked the Sunday roast? Who got up before anybody else to clean out the ashes from the fires and relight them?* I had even sawn logs. Sometimes I was so tired at the end of the day because everything on my to-do list had to be done. I rarely relaxed. *Why? Did it give me a sense of achievement, or did I feel that I was lavishing the love and affection on my family that I'd missed out on as a child?*

In those days I knew nothing about my needs, dreams, or aspirations. It didn't occur to me that there could be a life just for me. If anybody had asked me then what I'd like, apart from what I had, the answer would be, "I don't know." My whole life was just about being busy. There was no time for what I wanted, even if I knew what that was. Maybe that's why every day was so full of 'doing'. If I'd stopped to think, and then decided to pursue something outside my normal jobs I knew that my insecurities would show. I didn't want to be challenged or changed.

There were so many memories to bury coming back to Wiltshire. It was the place where as a sixteen-year-old I'd met my husband. The house where I now stayed was where I'd lived then. Little had changed, apart from circumstances. Is it possible to be mugged by your own memories? It certainly felt that way. The bells from the church that we were married in still pealed the same old tuneless peal from across the valley. Often on a Sunday morning before waking up properly I'd hear them and for a single moment I'd be transported back to my teenage years. The walks, smells, noises, and pubs were all the same forty years on. Every detail was so real: things that I can't believe I'd ever remember. I'd relive a scene from nearly four decades before, with every colour, smell, and feeling performed in front of me as if it were in the present. My mind played terrible tricks of what had happened during those years. I had no control over this process it seemed: as powerless to instigate it as I was to stop it. I recalled pictures of happier times and memories of things said. My self-esteem become as low as it could go, living my life fearful of failure because that was how I expected people would see me. It was an uncomfortable time.

Walking my sister's dogs I'd come across old haunts and wonder how I ended up here. It wasn't the easiest place to begin my recovery. One day, I passed my husband's old home and I wished that his mother was still alive. I wanted to knock at the door and tell her how I felt and she'd listen sympathetically. The old bench at the end of the lane was still there. My husband and I sat on it when we were courting. I'd first seen it when I was ten years old. It was strange being back there. The bench was rotten, but our initials were still carved on the base all these years later. It seemed like another reminder about my marriage – fallen apart and overgrown. I don't visit that bench any more. It can keep its memories.

Chapter 26 – Close to the edge

At the beginning of January 2007 I decided I needed some money, so looked for a job. I felt this would also stop me from going insane. I needed to get out of my current situation and find a fresh purpose. It would also give my family a bit of respite. I tried to keep out of the way as much as possible but I was always there and they had to listen to my constant ranting about the divorce. I made a concerted effort. I found an advertisement in the local newspaper for a job in catering, which was my forte. I applied and was successful in obtaining the position of catering assistant at a local college.

I started work at 7.15am and was paid a minimum wage. The job consisted of cooking large quantities of sausage, bacon, and eggs for the students' breakfasts, then food preparation for lunches. I'd wash up, mop floors, and clean everything including fat fryers and ovens, then finish mid-afternoon. I'd drive home smelling of chip fat. I'd cycled across Northern India, and yet here I was making myself a victim. A job on the minimum wage. *What was I doing?* I'd held down positions far senior to this. My self-esteem was taking a bashing. I was being driven down again. Rather than recovering, I was going backwards. After a few months I decided I was worth more and handed in my notice.

I was unemployed, had low self-confidence, and was still living with my brother. One day, I'd driven my sister up to the Crufts Dog Show in Birmingham. On arriving back at my sister's house and opening my post, I found a letter from my solicitor – more correspondence with regard to the divorce. It's not necessary to go into any details, but the contents of the letter were bad enough to send me over the edge. My sister reassured me that everything would be OK. I picked up my Sunday newspapers, plus my jacket, then told my sister that I was tired and going next door to my brother's house to have an early night. She saw me out with a peck on the cheek and wave. I started walking up the path towards my brother's house. It was a cold night for March, probably minus one or two. *Life just seemed so awful. What was the purpose of it?* I wasn't sure how much more I could take. I didn't feel that I wanted any more of it either.

Deciding not to go back to my brother's house, I walked down to the bottom of the estate, crying uncontrollably. I looked up and through the tears saw a rather frail elderly lady walking towards me, dressed only in a white short-sleeved cotton shirt and trousers. She was gripping a piece of broken wood about two feet long. I remember thinking at the time that I was seeing an apparition. *What else would you think?* She approached me and asked if I knew what number to call for the local police. She said that her husband had locked her out of the house and she'd tried to get in by breaking the door down, hence the piece of wood she was holding. I was in such a distressed state and felt myself getting annoyed with her. *Why are you giving me all this stuff when I can't deal with my own problems?* I rather rudely suggested she go to the local garage a few yards down the road and ask them. This could only happen to me. Just my luck to be getting geared up to top myself and run into an elderly lady brandishing a piece of wood! I felt very selfish when I found out later that this poor woman suffered with dementia. Her husband had actually died several years before.

I walked on past the garage and across a main road, where I came to the local pub. By this stage I was planning how I was going to kill myself, so decided that what I'd do was go into the pub and have a few stiff drinks to make it easier. On approaching the door, I thought, "Hang on a minute, I can't drink alcohol. I'm on antibiotics." This is a woman contemplating suicide. I continued walking further up the road, leaving the houses behind, and suddenly it was just fields. It was very dark by then, aside from the odd street light. I knew the area well. This particular lane was one my ex and I used frequently in our courting days to grab a quick kiss before returning back to our respective homes. It was yet another unwelcome reminder of the past. It was one more reason not to want to go on living.

The gate into one of the fields was ajar, so I entered, shoes crunching on the frosty grass. I walked to the middle of the field, where I proceeded to scream and scream. I needed that open space; I could never have shown such emotion in front of my family. I was too self-controlled to do that. I felt that I'd be letting myself down and showing that I couldn't cope, so my feelings became bottled up. All that pent-up anger and frustration exploded out of me. Luckily, there were no houses around otherwise I'd have probably had several police cars turning up. There was a large boulder nearby and I sat down to contemplate my next move. Realising how cold my rear end was, I placed the Sunday newspapers under me.

I decided the best possible way to top myself was an overdose. So, I walked swiftly back to the farm gate to locate the nearest street light. I rummaged through my handbag for anything I could swallow, only to find two paracetamols, a sea sickness tablet, and a screwed-up piece of silver paper with spent chewing gum inside! My mobile phone had been ringing constantly. My sister had realised after phoning my brother that I'd not arrived, and was very concerned about me. I didn't know there were search parties out. My brother went in one direction in his van, whilst my sister and her husband went in another.

The realisation of what I'd been thinking of doing was, by now, beginning to sink in. I was feeling so ashamed. How I could even contemplate such a thing as suicide. I hadn't taken into account what impact it would have had on my children and family – all I could think about was my own misery and hurt. Deep down I'd known that I didn't have the guts to do it, but something had to give, and it did. Feeling chilled to the bone, with a sore throat from screaming, I made my way back to the house.

I was greeted on my return by my family getting out of cars. My sister said, "Where the hell have you been? We've all been worried sick." I exploded, feeling totally out of control. I was angry and used words I wouldn't normally say, screaming, "Don't f*** ask!" I threw the Sunday newspapers on the pavement, then fled into my brother's house, slamming the door in their faces. How ungrateful was that? I was their guest, they'd been searching everywhere for me, and all I could do was shut them out. I rushed up two flights of stairs to my bedroom, removed my shoes, got into bed fully clothed, pulled the duvet up, and sobbed.

Everything had come to a head. It was all too much. No home, no marriage, no children near, and no money. My brother came up gingerly a little later with a mug of steaming tea and sat on the side of the bed with comforting words. Apparently my sister and sister-in-law had nominated him as spokesperson.

The following day I stayed in bed, still fully clothed but awake, until late morning. I felt embarrassed about my behaviour and wondered how to approach the family. Nobody dared to knock on my door for fear of being shouted at again.

I learnt so much from that experience. I believe it was the turning point for me. I told myself that I had two options: either slide back down into misery or keep on in the direction I was going. It had to be onwards and upwards. There really was no other choice. I'd done so well up to now. With support from friends and family, I managed to pull myself out of the mire. I started to move on again, reminding myself how far I'd come in such a short while. I was bound to have times like this. In fact, I was allowed to. After all, this wasn't just about the divorce, it was about so many other things as well: moving to a new country; new job; new house. Whereas before, I wouldn't have felt able to cope with all these challenges, now I was equal to the task and got on with it.

Chapter 27 – New house – new roots

As winter turned into spring I had a renewed sense of hope and looked forward. Everything around me felt a little better. Trees were turning green and bulbs pushed up. Even the birds sounded happier. There was so much to organise. It was only weeks before I moved into my new home and again I was wondering whether I could cope: after all I'd never bought a house before. *Would I be able to sort out all that I needed to on my own?* Doubt was creeping in as I went through the many things to do. Lists were everywhere of all the legalities and practicalities to complete.

In early May, sixteen months after our separation, the divorce still wasn't finalised. I was about to start living on my own again, missing that someone in my life who would help me deal with it. Now all the decisions were mine and it felt like it was too much. I'd no option but to get it done. After a few days I was actually enjoying it. I found the best deals, argued with the builders about snags in my new home, and I coped. Finally, moving day arrived. With the help of my family and friends, I was in my own home at last.

As the house was brand new I wondered whether I'd be able to make it cosy, but once my old pine kitchen table and dresser, bed, a few pictures, lamps, and tables had been arranged it began to feel like home. It was strange looking at all these things; once they'd been part of a home I'd shared with my husband. This was all that remained of that old life.

Having moved from the Island where there's rarely any crime I did worry about my security. *Would I spend nights listening out for every creak, wondering if I was being burgled or worse?* However, from the first night I spent there I always felt secure.

The views from the upstairs floor were wonderful. The front of my property overlooked the Marina. At night the houses that surrounded the Marina and the occupied boats moored there were illuminated and their reflections in the water gave a feeling of being somewhere abroad. From spring to early winter there was always something to watch. Excited families would board rented canal boats for holidays, accompanied by an instructor who explained to them the rules of the canal and basics of how to manoeuvre the large boat. I found it interesting watching their first attempts at three-point turns on a narrow canal and their mistakes.

There were also more experienced people who owned their boats. Some actually lived on them. They went past my window with their roofs laden with prams, bicycles, plant pots displaying colourful geraniums, and even little gardens. The wildlife on the canal is wonderful. A heron would perch itself on the end of a moored canal boat, watching the water intently to catch its next meal. There were also swans with their cygnets, ducks, even hawks. It's such a happy place to live.

My garden was tiny and completely enclosed. There was just enough space for a barbeque, a few chairs, several hanging baskets and tubs, a little wooden seat, garden shed (Soli's new home), and even a small raised bed to grow some organic vegetables. I was putting down roots, like my few flowers.

Chapter 28 – Clinics and computers

Once settled in my new home I needed to find another job. I applied for and obtained the position of part-time medical receptionist at a large medical centre about five miles from where I lived. Though I'd done similar jobs in the past, I knew this would be a real challenge because it was a paperless practice where everything was done via computer. I've never hit it off with them.

I worked twenty hours a week, including at one of the satellite surgeries in a village not far from the main surgery. The village was where my ex-husband was raised and his family had lived. This would be difficult for me. Elderly patients, some of whom I knew back in the sixties, were still around. Every time I came across someone from my past I had to deal with the awkwardness of explaining my situation.

After the excitement of getting the job, nerves started to kick in and I worried how I'd cope with the computer system. *Was I too old to learn?* Three weeks later, references and police checks done, I started work. There would be a few weeks' induction first. My uniform would take a while to arrive, so I was told to wear a black blouse and trousers. The one black blouse I owned I'd managed to shrink in my new washer/dryer, so it now gaped and on my first day, this wasn't a good look. I was told the idea in a surgery is to lower male blood pressure not increase it.

The second day was worse, computer training. It didn't help that I was being trained with someone else who'd started the same day. She was an absolute whizz kid. The last time I'd used a computer was seven months before, so I was feeling rather dithery and stupid, trying to keep up with what was going on, one hand on the mouse, the other holding my shirt together. I went home that day feeling really bad about myself. Over the next few weeks I was given training in every area that I might be working in. What had happened to the medical receptionist who just answered the telephone to make and cancel appointments? *Could my brain cope with this?* So much more was now involved. My head was exploding every night for weeks and I was going home exhausted.

After about six months I relaxed a little, still not completely confident, but nearly. By the eighth month, all of a sudden everything started to fall into place; at last I felt part of the team. I was enjoying the challenge every day brought. Something else I'd mastered – yeah!

Unfortunately, a couple of months after moving into my new house and starting the new job, my sister was diagnosed with breast cancer. I was totally devastated, and cried for hours. She underwent the operation followed by months of treatment. I did my best to support her as she'd supported me during the divorce.

After much discussion, my sister came up with a planting design for my little garden during her recuperation. As she came to the end of her treatment, we'd go to the local garden centres and started buying the plants: it was lovely, she was better, and my little garden was beginning to come together. I've always loved gardening and now with the help of my sister, we'd designed the layout that would make the most of the plants and the space.

Every time I came back from work and opened the gate, it was like entering a secret garden. The estate was full of new houses, a bit of landscaping dotted around, the odd tree, or fast-growing shrub, but on entering my little patch it was like being in a different world. For a garden that was less than eighteen months old it looked so well established, full of sweet smelling shrubs, colour everywhere, and lots of butterflies and bees. I was so proud of it. I even entered a garden competition and won first prize for the best small courtyard garden in the area. That was such a boost for my sister.

The competition judges had seemed particularly impressed by my recycling methods because dotted around my raised beds were yoghurt-pot slug traps filled with beer. Every three or four days I'd empty all the slugs into a large container and throw them into the Marina. The ducks loved them.

One day I was busy dead-heading some of the shrubs and whilst I was working on a bush in the corner, something hissed violently. It frightened me so much I nearly toppled backwards. Parting the leaves, I found a mallard duck on a nest. Several weeks later she hatched nine ducklings, and not knowing what to do next I contacted the local wildlife society to ask for advice. They told me that when Mum thought the ducklings were ready she'd lead them to water. If they went into the canal too soon, most of the ducklings would be eaten by pike. The garden was totally enclosed, apart from a gap under the front wooden gate which I nailed a piece of wood over. I bought special duck food and made them a swimming pool complete with diving board and ramp out of a paddling pool I bought for a few pounds. I nailed a diving board on to the side of a raised bed and put a piece of ply board into the pool at an angle, so they could get in and out.

As days passed, Mum, who I called Jemima, would go for her walk around my raised beds followed by the nine ducklings. Each time she came to a yoghurt pot full of beer and slugs she drank and ate readily. On arriving at the seventh pot, she toppled over onto the gravel. I felt terrible when I realised what the problem was – she was drunk! The yoghurt pots weren't refilled. Within a few days, the duck and ducklings had totally wrecked my beautiful garden. Everything was flattened, and all my organic lettuces had been eaten or covered in poo.

Enough was enough. With the help of my sister and brother-in-law, we managed to catch them all. If anybody had seen us that evening they'd have assumed we were mad. My brother-in-law managed to catch Jemima with a large fishing

net and placed her in a cat box. I fell into the ducks'
swimming pool when I was trying to catch them. We took the
ducks to a wildlife rescue centre.

Chapter 29 – Expanding horizons

The challenge for me now was learning to rejoice in this new world that I was constructing. After everything in my new home was more or less sorted out, life became a little hectic, in a nice way. It was a matter of what shall I do first now that I don't have anyone else to please? It was such a novelty. After the twenty hours I worked each week, I could do what I liked. I didn't want to hide away, so to distract myself from the fear of learning to be on my own I filled every single hour with things I'd always wanted to do. My life was now an endless succession of options, none of which had to be presented to a committee before being acted upon. At the beginning, this liberation was also bewildering.

My normal week consisted of belly dancing, writer's circle, drama group, painting and drawing classes. I did things I never imagined I could do, and loved every minute. One of my dreams was to join the local Amateur Dramatic Society. It was something I wouldn't even have contemplated doing years ago. With my newfound confidence, off I went one night to audition for a part in a production they were putting on called 'If Music Be the Food of Love'. Trust me to choose something with the word love in it. To my utter amazement, I got two small parts. The first of these was a scene from *Uneasy Money* by P. G. Wodehouse. It involved acting rather than singing, and me being kissed several times by another actor. I remember thinking I should not have had chilli for my dinner prior to the performance. Just before going on, waiting silently in the wings, I decided to grapple in my handbag to see if I could locate some mouth freshener. Unfortunately, it was pitch black in there and when I sprayed it into my mouth I started to choke and splutter, realising that it wasn't mouth freshener at all but lens cleaner.

My other role was singing a duet, 'Do You Love Me', from *Fiddler on the Roof*. I played Golde, singing to Tevye. In the story, Tevye and Golde are husband and wife who have been married for twenty-five years. This song was about Tevye asking Golde if she still loved him and Golde questioning whether she did. This part was made for me, considering what had happened. I was so scared, just me and the actor playing Tevye on stage. I felt completely at one with Golde's character and even shed a tear at the end of the song. After realising I could sing a little, I decided to also join a local choir.

My mind was exploding with conflicting feelings. I was trying to cram everything I ever wanted into my life as quickly as possible for fear time would run out. It was as if I'd made a mental list, and was working through it, ticking off everything as I achieved it. My home was becoming full of self-help books. I started a Transpersonal Psychology course up in Leicester. There was a thirst that I couldn't quench, wanting to find out as much as I could about how I ticked.

I always thought I was a fairly artistic person, over the years creating and decorating celebration cakes. I wondered if I could apply my talent elsewhere, so added to my list of 'to dos' painting and drawing. After attending a course for several weeks, I decided to take an 'Art and Pottery' holiday in Lyme Regis. Packing my case, I remember thinking this is going to be so liberating. It was the first time I'd gone on holiday on my own. I booked into a beautiful thatched guest house for bed and breakfast. The only sounds from the open window were bees humming and birds singing.

The three tutors that week were brilliant, so loose and flexible in their teaching. By the end of the week I was slapping paint on paper with abandon. We got up early one morning to paint the sun rising over the sea and it was certainly worthwhile. I made a few pottery pieces, and even went fishing to catch a mackerel, which I took back to the studio to paint its portrait before eating it later, grilled on the barbecue. By the time the week was up, I'd created not just one masterpiece but three. Well, they were masterpieces to me anyway. That week in Lyme helped me a great deal on my journey to find the 'me' I wanted to be.

About ten months after I'd moved into my new home, life was plodding along nicely, or so I thought. I was still in busy mode. I'd discovered so many interests that I wanted to pursue. Alongside work and hobbies I was attending college two mornings a week, doing courses in IT and English.

Chapter 30 – Body and brain

On Wednesday 26th March 2008 I was stopped in my tracks. I'd been having problems for a few weeks – terrible cough and when I tried to walk I became out of breath. This particular Wednesday I began to feel even worse. I climbed two flights of stairs at college, about to sit an English exam. On my arrival, I could hardly talk, trying desperately to catch my breath. Although I was feeling very unwell, I ignored my symptoms and completed the examination. I then made my way back to the car, my breathing getting so bad that I decided to drive straight to my doctor's surgery. The GP seemed a little concerned after checking my oxygen levels and proceeded to nebulise me several times, then informed me that she was calling an ambulance. I queried whether it was necessary, to which she replied that I had pneumonia and was a very sick woman. She enquired if there was anybody she could call on my behalf to accompany me to the hospital. My brother and sister-in-law arrived at the surgery and it was decided that my brother would drive my car back to the house. The ambulance arrived, and I was 'blue lighted' to the hospital. *What was happening?* I didn't think I was that ill, but I was. I should have listened to my body trying to tell me what state it was in, but I didn't.

As soon as I entered hospital everything changed. All of a sudden I had no control over my life whatsoever. It was awful. CAT scans, X-rays, drugs, ECGs, blood tests, and oxygen masks, then I was told that part of my lung had collapsed.

Even worse, twenty-four hours after being admitted to a respiratory ward it was closed because of a sickness and diarrhoea bug. None of the patients could be moved out and no visitors were allowed. One of my obsessions is hygiene, so all my worst fears were happening. I had to hover over the ward toilet rather than sitting for fear of catching something contagious. A sectioned patient came and sat on my bed:

filthy, smelly, and not wearing any underwear. Nurses had to change elderly patients' beds several times in the night due to soiling. The smell of faeces and vomit was suffocating. It was as if someone or something was testing me. It felt like I'd become a magnet to all my hang-ups and fears. I must have got through one and a half bottles of anti-bacterial liquid, washing my cutlery every time I ate. All my meals tasted of it, but at least I didn't catch that dreadful bug. Looking back, I'm sure that I had a reputation amongst the staff as a difficult patient. I even insisted that the nurses wash their hands before giving me my daily drugs. I must have been a nightmare. I was so determined that I wasn't going down with anything more than I already had. That was quite bad enough.

It's so strange why these episodes happen in one's life: at the time I just had to live through the hospital incident, but I learnt so much from it. I realised that I'm not invincible and it highlighted some of my worst fears. These experiences did make me slow down, reflect, and address several aspects of my behaviour. I realised that I must listen to my body and make a conscious effort to get my life back under control. Having allowed my enthusiasm to run away with me, my health had suffered. Moderation in all things was a lesson that I had to learn.

Chapter 31 – Interlude

Towards the end of June 2009, I received a most unexpected email from *This Morning* – Fern Britton was leaving the programme after ten years. A big party was being organised for her final show. It was also her fifty-second birthday the same day. Some of her more memorable moments were going to be highlighted. The India cycle ride was one of them and I'd been invited to attend. How wonderful to be included in such a special occasion. After numerous shopping trips to purchase the right outfit, I was on my way up to the studio. I was feeling good. It was great to be chauffeured around again and to be going back to one of the hotels I'd stayed at during my challenge.

The studio was decorated with balloons and banners. Tables covered with blue gingham cloths were loaded up with nibbles of all kinds. Fern knew there was to be a party, but didn't know who the invited guests were, of whom I was one. There were only three of us who weren't celebrities, so I felt very special. The surprise guests were kept well hidden during the show, but we were watching everything on the television monitors. After being miked up, a runner came to take us to the studio, where we waited in the wings. Eventually, Fern's husband Phil turned to her and said, "We have another surprise for you. Do you remember Jill who cycled across India with you?" Fern seemed delighted to see me. I recounted her 'losing it moment' when she threw her bike on the road. She laughed, as did everyone else in the studio.

As the programme proceeded, I was surrounded by more and more celebrities: John Barrowman, Michael Ball, Christopher Biggins, Matthew Kelly, Zöe Lucker, Jenny McAlpine, Jenny Eclair, to name but a few. When the programme went 'off air' the party carried on, champagne flowing. The runner who was supposed to let me know when my chauffeur arrived didn't 'run', he was decidedly the worst for wear and my poor chauffeur had to spend some time waiting for me downstairs. I was driven to Paddington Station and feeling more than a little wobbly, I was guided to the train.

I did get home!

Chapter 32 – Dating? Who me? No way! And then again...

I never expected to be single at the age of fifty-six. Now though, my lack of confidence and self-belief was persuading me that I could never be intelligent, funny, or pretty enough to make any man commit himself to me. *How would I meet him? Where was I going to find the courage to tell him my aspirations, hopes, and fears?* I'd been thinking about dating for a little while and was now ready to see what was out there.

The last time I'd dated was at the age of sixteen. Discussing this with women who'd also gone through divorce, it seemed most of them take one of three routes: either they throw themselves straight into another relationship, or they decide they hate men and will never trust another, or they take the self-discovery route. This is the direction I decided upon.

My sister read an advert in the local newspaper for a singles disco and said, "You ought to try that." Being a wimp, I decided there was no way I could go on my own, so I telephoned the contact number to ask if my married sister could come along for support. Initially they said no, but then agreed as long as she made it clear to any prospective suitors that she was married. It was being held at a function room in a village not far from us. On arrival, I decided it was probably not my sister's best idea, especially as outside the entrance hung a red light. After a few reassuring words from my sister, we parked the car and went in. Already I could see this was a big mistake. Dimmed lights, candles on rickety old tables, a small bar with several men propped up against it – or was it propping them up? One of these men seemed to be displaying a lopsided wig on his head.

There was a small dance floor, complete with disco in the corner. As I walked across the carpet in the direction of a lady sitting at a table with her cash box, my feet were sticking to the carpet. All a bit odd. After sending my sister to the bar to get the drinks – she's braver than me – we were discussing which one in the room I'd attract; if any. I said, "Knowing my luck it will be the guy with the rug on his head." To my horror, this man and his friend approached our table. My sister and I were close to hysterical laughter. If that wasn't enough his friend introduced himself with an intermittent stutter – the other holding his toupee on. Fearful of being chatted up, I said to my sister, "Do you fancy cutting a rug?" We excused ourselves for a dance. I'm afraid I couldn't put that any other way after seeing the lopsided wig on the gentleman's head. Fortunately, he didn't get the connection. We didn't stay long. I wondered if this was what life would be like now I was single. Sordid little function rooms with peculiar little men who looked like they'd been around the block a few times.

After that, I joined a singles organisation, thinking this would be a good idea, going out to lunch and trips to the theatre with people in a similar situation. The first meeting I went to was at a hotel not far from where I lived. It was pouring with rain, but I managed to park the car right outside. It was a very old-fashioned hotel and as I entered the foyer the receptionist informed me the group was meeting in a room just opposite reception. I was expecting to hear laughter or something but there was complete silence. I could even hear the tick of the pendulum clock in reception. On approaching the room where the meeting was being held, I wondered if I'd arrived too early, but when I went in I realised there were already about five people there. They were sitting in a circle, drinking tea. The place reminded me of a communal sitting room in a nursing home, complete with winged chairs covered in dull beige and grey heavily embossed floral material. Not a gin and tonic in sight!

I was watching the clock for the whole evening, wondering, for politeness sake, how soon I could leave. A couple of men

166

arrived in suits. I was wearing jeans and top: this was supposed to be an informal evening. Where was the fun and laughter? Where was their 'get up and go'; it looked as if it had 'got up and gone'. Some of this group were younger than me, yet sitting in that room drinking tea the idea of Zimmer frames didn't seem that illogical. Did I go there again? Not likely!

I don't remember ever allowing myself time in the past to find out how I ticked. Before going into another relationship there were so many things which I needed to address and understand. I had to learn first to love myself, warts and all. I was determined there was no way I was going to enter into another relationship making the same mistakes as I had in my marriage. After a few years on my own I was tiptoeing back into the dating scene. I was very lucky in having some support from the radio station BBC Wiltshire. It was rather strange how this came about.

One of the producers of the afternoon programme telephoned me. I'd done a little work with them after finishing the India trip and they'd kept in touch. They offered to help me find my 'ideal man'. Well, who could refuse that? They gave me free membership to an internet dating site. The next thing was to sort out my profile and picture, then to give me instruction on how to use the site. It was weird. What happened to the days of meeting someone in a coffee bar or behind the bike sheds at school? I was still sixteen in my head.

After being on the site for twenty-four hours I logged in for the first time to see what was happening. A bit of a shock awaited me. There had been sixty views of my profile, fifteen winks, and three e-mails. I was somewhat surprised to receive so many compliments and felt rather flattered by all the attention, especially at my age. I was a little confused also, as one of the winks was from a woman. Not just that, I was being winked at by men whose ages ranged from twenty-one to eighty. *Surely a twenty-one-year-old was looking for a mother, and the eighty-year-old?* Well, he probably winked at me and within ten minutes had forgotten he'd winked at all. This was a little disconcerting I must admit and as usual I tried to analyse why men so much younger would look at a much older woman, instead of just accepting that they might.

It was extremely difficult to get to know someone via email. It seemed so impersonal, but after a short while I became a dab hand at sending messages. The first one took me at least an hour to compose.

I'd been corresponding with a gentleman for a few weeks via email when we agreed to exchange mobile numbers and have a chat. We eventually decided to meet. I felt rather nervous, wondering if he'd lied about himself in his profile. Was he much older, maybe he had bad teeth, or worse was a serial-rapist? I thought it would be best to meet at lunchtime.

The presenter from BBC Wiltshire offered to come with me and hide behind a palm tree or something, but that would probably have made me feel even more nervous so I declined this offer. Instead a rendezvous with the gentleman was arranged in a local pub. I asked him if he wanted me to wear a white carnation in my hair so that he could identify me. There was no response to that comment and I realised then that he didn't have much of a sense of humour. I decided to still meet him though and drove to the pub in question. It felt a little like going for a job interview. The gentleman concerned had already arrived and was waiting for me in the car park. He was slightly younger than me but first impressions were OK. He opened the door for me leading into the restaurant. Good start I thought, he gained his first point. We were seated at a small table by the window. There was time for some small talk before my soup arrived but being so nervous I was unable to look at him, and proceeded to talk to my leek and potato soup, not able to give this poor man eye contact.

He wasn't the one for me and as he walked me back to the car I wondered what was expected. Would he shake my hand, give me a peck on the cheek, or maybe a full mouth to mouth kiss? As we arrived at my car I got in rather quickly before he got too close and wound the window down about six inches, just enough for him to say goodbye. I think he got the message. I wondered whether things would get better and after several dates with different men I gained a little confidence, working my way up from talking to my soup to talking directly to the man's chest. With my confidence improving I even got a little higher and managed to talk to a picture over my date's right shoulder. As time went on, I gained more confidence, and I even noticed myself giving them a bit of eye contact.

My understanding of men and how they ticked was helped enormously through using the site. I started to identify which men were no-nos. Profiles without pictures – why would you talk to someone who doesn't show a picture? What were they hiding? Were they men just looking for a good time, nothing else, or men still married just wanting to see what life was like single? Some of the profile pictures were scary. One such photograph which was attached to a rather racy email I opened up late one evening. The picture looked like a police mug shot. All that was missing was an identification number. I was so freaked out I found myself going around the house checking that all the doors and windows were locked. I even looked under the beds and inside wardrobes.

Sometimes men lied about their age, height, and weight. The whole experience of meeting someone from a profile online can be very false. I was mainly pursued by balding dwarves with halitosis. Superficial, I know, and easily remedied with lifts in the shoes and a good breath freshener.

I was extremely worried about a new relationship, especially if it advanced to the physical stage. Whilst talking to these potential partners, I got the distinct impression I wasn't the only one worried about moving on. These men, well some of them, had met women who after just one date expected them to go home to have sex. Some of the men seemed to want a more platonic, caring, emotional relationship. I actually felt sorry for them; how awful to have this obligation to 'perform'. No wonder they doubted their masculinity if put under that sort of pressure. Meeting these men changed my perspective of relationships. I learnt so much. My generation's expectations of a woman's behaviour were no longer relevant.

I used to be afraid of what my parents might say about a prospective suitor, or how I behaved. Now, my only problem was how my children would perceive a future partner of mine. Would they be embarrassed, confused, or even threatened by my relationship with another man? When I told them I was going out, the response was almost that of a parent. *Where are you going? What time will you be back? Are you sure you're going to be safe?* For goodness sake, I'm sixty! For me the most important lesson I've learnt from this isn't to take life seriously, just enjoy meeting new people.

One day I thought I'd found my prince. A forty-six-year-old came into my life, fourteen years my junior, and he was rather nice. I tried to make myself look the best I could. I made an appointment with my niece, a beautician, who always keeps her aunt in perfect condition. I let her loose with the wax! Eye brows, eye lashes, and legs waxed, I came out looking like a plucked chicken.

I wondered how I'd cope if a physical relationship with him developed. *Would I place sticky tape under my breasts to make them look pert? Would I need a flow chart pinned to the back of the bed with arrows guiding me to the next move? Maybe a can of WD40 would be useful? Could I breathe in long enough to keep my tummy tucked in for the duration and how could I preserve my make-up and hair to look perfect the next morning? Would he hold a score card up out of ten?* This was all so frightening. I wondered if riding across India was easier.

Alas, the forty-six-year-old didn't last and we never got to that stage. A meeting with his mates, a few pints down his throat to loosen his tongue, he told them he was going out with a sixty-year-old woman. They gave him a ribbing, "You can do better than that, mate. Fancy going out with an OAP!" How awful to be judged on age alone. They hadn't even seen a picture and knew nothing about me, yet they could make a decision just on age. How harsh was that? He didn't phone.

I rang him the next day. He said he hadn't called because he couldn't make up his mind what to do, saying he really liked me but couldn't come to a decision after what his friends had said. So I made the decision easy for him, by telling him if he was worried about what his mates said then he wasn't the man for me. I'd loaned him some pictures to brighten up the walls as he was trying to sell his house. These were returned the following day and left in the garden inside charity bags marked 'Help the Aged'! A little pointed, I thought.

Drowning my sorrows, I drank a whole bottle of Pinot Grigio. Getting up the next day with a bit of a hangover, I thought I had something to prove, so 'Soli' came out of the shed. Wearing a fluorescent yellow T-shirt, cycling shorts, gloves, and helmet, I proceeded to cycle the twenty-five miles to Bath and back. Considering it was the first time I'd cycled in a year, I thought that's not bad. Later that day I attended a Salsa workout class, and all this with a hangover. Well guys, that's an OAP for you!

Chapter 33 – Sixty is only a number!

I'd reached the age of sixty – a pensioner and going into old age. I believe the fear of ageing comes from lives that have not found any meaning. Once a week there's some sort of bad news and once a month, a funeral. People who seem extremely fit, run miles a day, and eat only fresh fruit and nuts suddenly drop dead. People who drink a bottle of wine and smoke sixty cigarettes a day drop dead. It seems to make no difference. You're suddenly taking part in a lottery. I'm beginning to look at people of my age, consciously assessing their apparent state of health and fitness. *Am I deteriorating like them? Do I really look that old?* They seem shorter than they were. They complain their hands, knees, shoulders, hips, and back have gone. They tell me that they take so many pills they rattle. Any new conversation we have seems to be centred on CAT scans and MRIs. Everywhere I look there's cancer. *Am I fooling myself? Am I like that?* I didn't think I was, but now I notice that this age thing is trying to pull me down. *Why can't I eat what I like any more?* Just thinking about a bowl of chips makes me gain weight. Why, when I run my hands under a hot air dryer in the ladies' toilet, does my skin leave my bones and wrinkle up like sand rippling across a desert in a gentle wind? Everybody gets old and dies. It's life and we can't control that. What I can do is to decide how I spend the precious time I have left and by golly I'm going into old age kicking and screaming!

I decided that my sixtieth was the birthday I would organise myself. I know my family would have put on a good spread, but this was something I needed to do alone. I recognised at last that I deserved to spoil myself, so to everyone's surprise I booked a cruise to the Caribbean. In April 2010 I flew out to Barbados to join the ship 'Oceana' for my holiday. In fourteen days I visited the beautiful islands of St Lucia, St Maarten, Tortola, Antigua, and Madeira before cruising back to Southampton across the Atlantic Ocean. The ship was magnificent, a floating five-star hotel, fantastic food, and wonderful entertainment. I was travelling alone, but did have friends I knew on the ship. Although I had the freedom to do what I liked, it was nice to meet them for dinner.

I joined the 'Oceana' choir and took part in several of the on-board activities and watched some fantastic shows in the evenings. There was coffee arranged for single travellers to meet on the mornings we were at sea and the stewards were always asking us if there was something that we, as single travellers, were missing out on whilst on board. I said I loved dancing and would love to go clubbing. They said that wasn't a problem, and to look in the daily *What's On* magazine in twenty-four hours' time, which I did. I couldn't believe what they'd done. It was highlighted, 10.00pm until late at the 'Le Club' nightclub, 'Come Jiggle with Jill'. Well the connotations that threw up were not about dancing! I went along somewhat apprehensively. Four men jumped up on the floor asking for a jiggle. I answered, "I hope it's dancing you're talking about here." A good night was had by all.

There were five formal dress nights for dinner. Prior to the cruise I went on a shopping spree and bought some dresses. I don't do dresses. One of the evening events was a formal black and white dress code. I showered and put on my black silk and chiffon evening gown, with new black stilettos. I looked at myself in a full-length mirror and began to cry. I realised, for the very first time in my life, that I looked feminine and, although difficult to say, even attractive. How sad was this? It had taken me all that time to see I was actually OK. Sixty years of self-deprecation. No wonder it hit me so hard looking in that mirror.

Back home, I also organised a big party on the day of my actual birthday. Usually, I'd have done the catering myself, but not this time. The party I wanted was an informal gathering of family and friends. I really wanted a good rock band, so over several weeks my sister and I went out scouting. It was such good fun. We found the most amazing band called 'Straight Shooter' and after a fair bit of juggling on their part, they played at my party.

My daughter made me a birthday cake consisting of ninety-six cupcakes, one for each of the guests, arranged on a tiered frame. It looked fabulous. Fish and chip suppers all round as well. It was a really good night. Most of those who came were people I'd met after the divorce, so comparing that with my fortieth birthday, where most of those people were my husband's friends, was very satisfying. This was all down to me and my new life. I enjoyed my sixtieth.

Chapter 34 – Up and down

It hasn't all been a bed of roses. My life was settling down nicely but just two years after my sixtieth I came down with a huge bump again.

I was on holiday in Tenerife, but during my stay I ended up being admitted to hospital with bronchitis.

After returning to England I began to feel really unwell; again I found myself being admitted to hospital, with pneumonia again.

I spent nine days in intensive care. The family were called and informed how seriously ill I was, and told to expect the worst. But I pulled through, and after spending twelve days in hospital and feeling as weak as a kitten, I was allowed home. It took me quite a while to get back on my feet and functioning properly again.

I realised during this time how important family really are.

Having had to care for, and to a large extent, bring up my two daughters single handed, I have many precious memories of these days. Even now a single memory or thought can be enough to cause emotion to well up from deep inside and put me back to a place or time in my past when my daughters were young. They were my focus, my life, my world, and gave me reason to love life with them and live it to the full.

I gave them love and they returned it a thousand times over. They made me laugh and cry. They made our house a proper home with their chatter and noise. One minute clinging to me for dear life as toddlers and then pushing me away when they became teenagers. Seeing them take part in stage productions and wishing that I could have done that when I was their age, but it was not available to me. Holding my breath that they did not forget their lines, and knowing all of them myself because we had rehearsed them together. Going shopping, reading each other's moods and thoughts, and not needing words to express them.

They have become my best friends and we have learnt so much from each other. The three of us know that we are allowed choices in this world and they have helped me to make mine and supported the ones that I have made, even some of the not so good ones. In the past, especially the times when I was so alone with just the children and a husband many miles away for so long, these two were an inspiration and I lived through, and for them.

I feel that all of these experiences have helped my daughters develop into lively and stimulating companions and they know that I enjoy their company when we meet now. How different from my own upbringing where such openness and closeness were frowned upon. We have a true sense of connection and an ongoing and developing relationship, something that I never had with my parents. I have the joy of seeing them acting in a way that I taught them and passing this on to my grandchildren – I hear myself from years ago and my own mannerisms are mirrored in their actions. I must have got something right for they make me so proud of them and their achievements. They have made all the things that I did, and the sacrifices that I made, worth so much more and because of that, my life is so much richer.

After I was taken so seriously ill with pneumonia and very nearly died, their feelings for me were shown very clearly and our relationships became even closer. Tenderness and raw emotion came to the surface and although I knew that they loved me, they let me see just how much I meant to them. Maybe it was because they thought I was going to die that let their natural barriers down – they were grown women, married and with their own problems – but they showed me that I was still their Mum and that they did not want to lose me. Tables were turned; they had always been the centre of attention but now it was me. I was not used to that and it took me by surprise at just how much they showed their feelings for me. They were coming into the hospital with pots of cream for my skin, massaging my swollen feet and hands, producing frozen lollies to help me eat after that horrid tube down my throat had finally been removed, ensuring that I had all that I needed.

They were giving back to me all that I had given to them over the years – my girls were now giving their hearts to me: wasn't it always my place to give mine to them? Now, as well, they were giving me the will to live.

Is there anything more that children can give to their mother?

Chapter 35 – Still onwards

How grateful and thankful I am that I've been given this second chance at life, and what a life it will be. I'm now at a stage where I feel happy and at ease with myself, no longer living in the shadows of other people's lives. I cast my own shadow at last. I feel I have now become my own cherished soul mate. I see myself for who I am, warts and all. I still quite like me. I can now decide what I want to do, not bow to others' wishes or my perception of their needs. I'm totally at ease in all kinds of company and I no longer take people at face value.

Several years have now passed since starting the book, and I've only just got around to finishing the last chapter. Putting a cover on it would be a closure of a very sad part of my life.

My forays into internet dating have finally paid off. I've found a wonderful man, called Stewart. We corresponded by email through one of the sites for a few years as friends. We were both involved in other relationships and lived too far away to meet each other, even if we'd been inclined to do so. Eventually, our situations both changed and his job brought him closer to where I was living. After a few chats, we decided to meet. We hit it off and we were married in 2015. My life couldn't be any happier. What a caring, loving man he is.

I had Stewart by my side the first time I saw my ex-husband after several years at a family christening. It would have been so difficult without Stewart. We walked into church together; Stewart introduced himself to my ex and shook his hand. This broke the ice and things were civil for the rest of the day. I'd worked myself into such a frenzy leading up to the day where I'd come face to face with my ex, but things worked out so much better than I'd imagined. Stewart made a lovely comment, ''His loss and my gain.'' That cheered me up. We had a lovely afternoon.

Sadly, I lost another dog, Fidget. I'd had him in my life for such a short time. At the age of just five, he was diagnosed with cancer. He deteriorated quickly, and within eight weeks of becoming ill, the very difficult decision was made to have him put to sleep. What a special wee boy he was, and my life was better for having known him. In the past, when there were days I had no one to go home to, he was there to greet me, tail wagging.

So, happy ever after? All in all, yes. I've discovered a completely different side of me which I feel sure I'd always suppressed, never allowing it to surface. Most importantly, I no longer feel like a ventriloquist's dummy: I have a voice of my own. I finally learnt that I'm an equal to anybody. I have my strong points and my weaknesses, but so does everybody else. There's nothing wrong in admitting that you have made a mistake; it's denying it that's so destructive.

Stewart and I bought a house together and moved in to fix it up three months prior to our wedding. The house had been on the market for nearly six months. It was in a rundown condition, and I'm sure people would have viewed the property and either not seen its potential or thought that too much work was needed. Luckily, we didn't mind the challenge involved to get the house into the home we wanted it to be. Stewart loves DIY and is very good at it, able to turn his hand to just about anything. Almost immediately after we moved in Stewart gutted the place – painting, decorating, new carpets and floors.

The house had a smallish kitchen and dining room directly next to it, and we'd discussed knocking the wall down between the two to create a bigger kitchen. Just four weeks before the wedding Stewart decided to do just that! I went shopping, and on my return the wall was gone. The house was full of dust and debris. I wasn't happy. A dear friend who was helping me make our wedding cake luckily offered her dust-free kitchen so I could to finish it there.

However, by the time the wedding arrived the DIY was

sorted, and the house was looking much more like we wanted it to be.

We had a lovely wedding day. Stewart had arranged a lovely surprise for me – I was going to be chauffeured to the wedding in a 1927 vintage car. Little did he know it was hardly roadworthy! It arrived at our house. My brother was giving me away, and we climbed into the back of the car. It had started to rain quite heavily, so I said that we should shut the windows. It turned out that they were open for a reason. My brother's comment was, "If we close the windows we will be dead before we get there!" Like any old car it smoked a bit, but I think he exaggerated the effect! We arrived early. The chauffeur said we'd have to get out in the rain, because if he stalled the car it might not start again, so the registrar had to come out early to check my details. In the end we were married before I should have even got there.

Everything went beautifully though; the car came back to take us to the reception. It had to go up a hill on the way, and on an especially steep part was misfiring and nearly stalled. It got us to the reception, although I think it would have been quicker to walk, but still a lovely thought, Stewart.

The reception and evening event went fantastically, and we enjoyed being with our family and close friends.

Fifteen months after losing Fidget and a lot of soul-searching, I decided to get another Blue Roan Cocker Spaniel puppy. We have named him Dibble and he's an absolute joy.

We've been married for nearly four years now, and time moves on. Life still throws up issues that are difficult to deal with at times, and I'm sure it always will. Unfortunately, my dear sister, Jackie, died in May 2018. She was by my side whilst I was going through this terrible time. There's now a big void in my life where Jackie was. For as long as I can remember, apart from holidays, I spoke to her at least once a day for a chat and I miss that so much.

It was two years after our separation that I decided to

begin writing this book. I found I had to stop quite frequently, to take myself away. It was a bit like going through therapy, some days replaying all those terrible times, feeling the pain all over again. It was like a traffic jam going on in my head. It was full of thoughts and feelings, conscious and unconscious, all baying for attention. The worst bit of all was that the recollections were in no particular order. Luckily, I had kept diaries throughout this terrible time, and this book is based on those. I was being mentally overwhelmed, turning every thought and feeling over and over. Days felt wasted. One minute it was early morning, the next late afternoon. *What had I done in that time?* I was getting totally distracted by my thoughts, one minute washing dishes, the next frantically writing notes to myself to add bits to the book. Sometimes I felt thoughtful, then sad. I'd be completely exhausted for the rest of the day. There were things I had to force myself to bring up, preferring them to stay deep down, never to be revisited. My home got dustier, shopping sometimes not done. I felt very reclusive at times. As thoughts tumbled into my head I needed to get them on to paper for fear they'd disappear back into that traffic jam, never to resurface.

Through coping with this awful time in my life I believe that I learnt so much about myself and started to grow. It was the way I began to process those feelings that made the difference. Sometimes this journey of self-awareness has been very difficult. I didn't ask for it to happen, it just did. There were times when I wished that I'd never started this journey, but then I'd realise how far I'd come. There's no way I'd want to turn back now.

I've been told that I've changed as a person. I no longer wear 'The Face' any more, as I did in my past life. I'm still a giver, but on my own terms now, not because I ought to be, but because I want to. Stewart is a giver too. I know he'd do anything for me. I value my life more than ever, and try to enjoy something every day if I can. Stewart is my rock and I love him. I needed a more intimate relationship and I found that with him. One of the lovely things to come out of our marriage is that now we have six grandchildren between us – two girls and four boys, ranging from two and a half to fifteen. How wonderful is that?

Author Acknowledgements

I wouldn't have been able to write this book without enormous help from the following people and my grateful thanks goes to them. If I've missed anybody by name, please forgive me, but know that I am so grateful!

To both my daughters and their long-suffering husbands for all that they have had to cope with throughout the last few years.

To my dear sister Jackie, for her love and support. She took my first scribblings and got them into some sort of order for me as well as trying to sort out my head!

To Laurie and Karen for giving me shelter, warmth, and love when I most needed it.

To Sam, my homeopath and friend on the Isle of Man and his better half Pat, who gave me the insight into what I could become, plus remedies and encouragement. In that order!

Thanks to Lynne, for taking the time to proofread my book. Not an easy thing to do.

To Holly, my friend in Wiltshire, who was determined that I should finish this. Thank you for your support and help.

To Sharon and Fiona for getting my initial scribblings on to the computer. How they read my handwriting I just don't know!

My thanks to Clive and Anne for helping me bring this book to fruition.

To Fern Britton for all the help and support she gave me and for giving me the chance to take part in challenges that helped me to change my life.

Thank you, Julie Dawn Cole, for getting me fit and just being there when it mattered most, and for permission to use the poem *Cycle India 2006*.

To all the team at *This Morning*, not forgetting my chauffeurs.

To all the great group of girls that were chosen to take part in 'The Challenge of Your Life'.

To all those brave ladies who took part in the Women for Women cycle across India. What would I have done without you? Thank you for your support.

To Classic Tours, who organise worldwide charity challenges.

To Ian Scrannage for his wonderful cover illustration.

To BBC Wiltshire for helping me to find my 'Knight in Shining Armour'.

And lastly to Stewart for finding me and making me the person I've always wanted to be and making me feel so loved and wanted. Thank you from the bottom of my heart.

Lightning Source UK Ltd.
Milton Keynes UK
UKHW011846270520
363993UK00001B/30

9 781999 884246